Pra

The Gospel

MW01282822

"Jeff and I are thankful the Lord has provided more gospel-centered Enneagram teachers like Tyler Zach. Whether you are new to the Enneagram or have studied it for years, we know that you'll find lasting value in this book. On these pages, Tyler's creative wisdom shines, and his focus always remains on Jesus."

— Beth & Jeff McCord, co-founders of Your Enneagram Coach, best-selling authors of *Becoming Us: Using the Enneagram to Create a Thriving Gospel-Centered Marriage*

"'Do you realize that others can see God more clearly through your personality?' While that quote lacks the full context of Tyler Zach's reflection on Genesis 1, the question itself stopped me in my tracks. It's one example of many throughout his writing that provoke reflection for a Type 1 like me. But more than reflection, the insightful writing and use of Scripture helped me grow. Tyler simply, beautifully, and clearly weaves God's Word, pointed questions, personality insight, and also the grace-filled message of the gospel that can help you grow as well. Thanks for writing a great devotional Tyler!"

— Dr. Todd Engstrom, executive pastor of The Austin Stone

"This devotional confirmed and affirmed everything that God has been speaking into me and all that therapy has been teaching me in this season. No matter where you are in your healing journey as a Type 1, this devotional has immense value for you. Tyler writes with such care, awareness, and intentionality that leaves you feeling incredibly seen and understood."

— Dayo Ajanaku, founder of @TheBlackEnneagram

"I've read each of Tyler's devotionals so far and have loved the way he writes with such empathy and encouragement in every single one of them. But as a Type 1 myself, this latest devotional struck a new and beautiful chord. Tyler has a gifted way of edifying and empowering us to move toward grace in new and fresh ways."

— **Kim Eddy, author of *The Enneagram for Beginners: A Christian Guide to Understanding Your Type for a God-Centered Life***

" ... A personalized devotional for your personality type. I love it! ... "

— **Les Parrott, Ph.D., #1 *New York Times* bestselling author of *Saving Your Marriage Before It Starts***

" ... an extraordinary gift to all Enneagram enthusiasts ... "

— **Marilyn Vancil, author of *Self to Lose, Self to Find: Using the Enneagram to Uncover Your True, God-Gifted Self***

" ... Journey through these pages to remember who you are and how to bring your best self to a world in need. ... "

— **Drew Moser, Ph.D., author of *The Enneagram of Discernment: The Way of Vocation, Wisdom, and Practice***

" ... clear, compelling, and beyond profound."

— **John Fooshee, president of People Launching and Gospel Enneagram**

The Gospel for Improvers

A 40-Day Devotional for
Honest, Responsible Perfectionists

BY TYLER ZACH

To Kelsey, my younger sister, who is very responsible, extremely hardworking, fiercely empathetic, mature beyond her years, and, of course, always right!

Table of Contents

Foreword

WHEN JEFF AND I FIRST DISCOVERED THE Enneagram, it wasn't easy finding books written from a Christian worldview. We understood how important Gospel-centered Enneagram resources could be, and that inspired us to start our business, Your Enneagram Coach. Since then, we've helped over one million people find their Type through our free assessment and grow through our online classes, coaching certifications, books, and podcast.

Upstanding and responsible, Type 1s always strive to do what they view as right. They walk through life focused on the way things should be and seek to improve everything around them. As a Type 9, I have a Type 1 Wing. This connection brings accuracy and precision to my teaching and coaching. Your Enneagram Coach wouldn't be what it is today without my 1 Wing. It kept me principled and focused on doing what was right – bringing a Gospel-centered Enneagram to people to show them what's wrong so that Christ can fix it!

The Enneagram is a tool that clarifies our fallen nature while also reminding us we are created in the *Imago Dei* ("image of God"). When Jeff and I understood the why behind our thoughts and actions, it transformed how we looked at ourselves, our relationship with God, our marriage, our parenting, and (obviously) our careers. Taking a risk by starting a business was both exciting and terrifying. We could have easily spun out of control or run out of gas (at times, we did!), but knowing the Enneagram, as seen through the lens of the gospel, kept us grounded and on track.

The world needs Type 1s because you bring out the best in others. Your self-discipline, focus, responsibility, and principles make the world better. In uncertain times, you provide a stable foundation, serving others with patience and integrity, and guiding them towards goodness.

Like all numbers, Type 1s can have seasons of struggle. Your Inner Critic is extremely hard on you, making you feel that what you do is never good enough. To appease this voice, you often take on too much responsibility and feel resentment that you can't relax and have fun. The Enneagram can help you quiet the voice of your Inner Critic so you can rest in the voice of the Holy Spirit. Type 1s, we are confident that this 40-day devotional will guide you toward a more peaceful and carefree YOU.

Jeff and I are thankful the Lord has provided more gospel-centered Enneagram teachers like Tyler Zach. Whether you are new to the Enneagram or have studied it for years, we know that you'll find lasting value in this book. On these pages, Tyler's creative wisdom shines, and his focus always remains on Jesus. We're praying that God will meet you on these pages, and you will recognize your inherent value as His beloved child.

Jesus is the author and perfecter of our faith (Hebrews 12:2). He finished the great task He set out to do (John 19:30). A vital part of His ministry was to stay in alignment with His Father, and He did this by setting aside time for rest and reflection. He invites you to do the same, to come away, to separate from the crowds, and BE with Him. Remember, you are loved and valued for simply being you. You do not have to gain Christ's approval. You are accepted right now as you are.

—Beth and Jeff McCord
co-founders of Your Enneagram Coach
best-selling authors of *Becoming Us: Using the Enneagram to Create a Thriving Gospel-Centered Marriage*

Introduction:

The Gospel for Improvers

YOU DON'T HAVE TO BE PERFECT TO BE PERFECTLY LOVED. A book like this won't help you to be loved any more (or less) than you are right now. Though the Table of Contents makes for a great self-improvement checklist, the truth is you can't do anything to improve on God's love and respect for you.

Rather than an agenda for self-improvement, consider this book an invitation to make a conscious effort every day to get off the hamster wheel—to push pause on improving the world long enough to sit at the feet of Jesus and remind yourself you are loved for *whose* you are, not *what* you improve. No one understands you like your heavenly Father does: He sees every question you ask, every concern you make, and every detail you want clarified as all coming from a place of love to make this world a better place. He also knows you are harder on yourself than on anyone else. He gets you! Therefore, let this be your daily motto: *God's love first, then improvements.*

Make no mistake: This is not one of those fluffy devotionals that is so inspirational it's no earthly good. Though the blue cover of this book was chosen to represent the sky-high dreams you have for the world—no one can match your idealism and drive to return to our native purity—the truth is, we will get very practical.

Over the next 40 days, I want to come alongside to help you *actualize* your full potential, *bring clarity* to who you are and where you can go, and *tap into* that ideal vision you have to restore the brokenness of the world until it is made whole again. I want to *give you hope* if you are feeling overwhelmed, which includes helping you identify what you're *not* responsible for. As the Serenity Prayer (a.k.a. The Improver's Prayer) goes, "God, grant me the serenity to accept the things I cannot change, courage to change the things I can, and wisdom to know the difference."[1] I want to *help you enjoy every moment* without having to evaluate it, and see all of life as a thrilling journey filled with spontaneous surprises, laughter, optimism, and deep curiosity. Get ready to have God redefine your definition of *good* and reorient your version of the "good life" to something beyond your comprehension or control.

The Enneagram can be a helpful and necessary tool for spiritual growth through self-awareness. Unlike other personality profiles, the aim of the Enneagram is to uncover why we do what we do—to help us see what lies behind our strengths and weaknesses. If we use this as a diagnostic tool, allowing the Bible to provide the language for our interpretation, then the Enneagram can produce great change in our lives, relationships, and work.

This is a book about Enneagram types, but don't be mistaken. Fundamentally, I'm a pastor who believes the Bible is the inspired Word of God and is sufficient for all He requires us to believe and do. That said, I also believe God has provided additional insights in fields like medicine and psychology that are helpful in understanding the incredible world God has made. We must tread carefully as we draw insights from fields with limited horizons of evidence like psychology (we still have so much more to learn about the brain!), and as with anything we come across in this fallible world, we can put on our gospel lens and make use of the wisdom God has poured out on the whole human race.

What Makes This Book Different?
While there are other projects explaining the Enneagram, the primary aim of this book is to go deeper by applying the truth of God's Word specifically to your type over the next 40 days. If you are suspicious of the Enneagram or know someone who is, download my free resource called *Should Christians Use The Enneagram?* at gospelforenneagram.com. I pray it will help you engage with the Enneagram as a Christian, and then talk about it with others.

Before we get to the daily devotions, let's look at how the gospel both affirms and challenges the unique characteristics of your type.

---

1 Crosswalk Editorial Staff, "The Serenity Prayer: Full Version, Author, and Bible Meaning," Crosswalk.com, June 17, 2020. https://www.crosswalk.com/faith/prayer/serenity-prayer-applying-3-truths-from-the-bible.html.

The Gospel Affirms Improvers

God sympathizes with the worldview of an Improver. This chaotic world lacks order in many ways and is filled with irresponsible, unethical, and careless people. We need honest, sincere Improvers who will take responsibility and follow through, show us how to be mature adults living in a culture of prolonged adolescence, teach us how to do things correctly and with complete integrity, and demonstrate a *faith that works*. Therefore, an Improver will be happy to know the Bible affirms the following beliefs:

- **God created us to bring order.** "For God is not a God of disorder but of peace."[2]

- **God created us to be disciplined and hardworking.** "And let us not grow weary of doing good, for in due season we will reap, if we do not give up."[3]

- **God created us to be honest and reliable.** "One who is faithful in a very little is also faithful in much, and one who is dishonest in a very little is also dishonest in much."[4]

- **God created us to have high standards.** "You therefore must be perfect, as your heavenly Father is perfect."[5]

- **God created us to be conscientious**. Jesus said, "For I have come down from heaven, not to do my own will but the will of him who sent me."[6]

- **God created us to live with integrity.** "Whoever walks in integrity walks securely, but he who makes his ways crooked will be found out."[7]

- **God created us to be good examples.** "Brothers, join in imitating me, and keep your eyes on those who walk according to the example you have in us."[8]

---

2   1 Corinthians 14:33 NIV

3   Galatians 6:9

4   Luke 16:10

5   Matthew 5:48

6   John 6:38

7   Proverbs 10:9

8   Philippians 3:17

The Gospel Challenges Improvers

The gospel also provides specific challenges to Improvers. Now we'll explore the most common lies Ones believe and see how the Bible provides much better promises and blessings. We will move deeper into each of these throughout the next 40 days.

- **Lie #1: Perfection is attainable.** The primary focus of attention of Improvers typically goes to errors or what's wrong. Even when you are not seeking out mistakes, they jump out at you and scream for your attention. This leaves Ones chronically frustrated with the way things are. As a result, Ones work tirelessly to bring order to chaos. But serenity, the One's virtue, is not something that can be achieved through hard work; it's received through union with Christ. The peace of Christ will guard you from being assaulted by the world's imperfections.[9] Finding serenity, that inward felt sense of goodness and wholeness, doesn't hinge on improved circumstances, but on relaxing in God's presence and trusting that He is in sovereign control of all things. Serenity doesn't turn a blind eye to what needs improving but allows you to enjoy the world as it is because things don't need to be perfect to be in the presence of love.

- **Lie #2: I must be perfect to be good.** God created the world and saw that it was "very good"[10]—but Improvers are tempted to say, "I must be perfect to be good." Therefore, they make an idol out of perfection, clinging to a merit-based system through which they can earn their righteousness and avoid their greatest fears of being wrong, bad, unredeemable, or condemned. Thankfully, the gospel says you are accepted not because your worth is tied to your goodness, but in Jesus Christ, the Perfect One. And whatever goodness you feel you still lack has been fully credited to your account: "For our sake he made him to be sin who knew no sin, so that in him we might become the righteousness of God."[11]

- **Lie #3: I can't make any mistakes.** The childhood message that Improvers received was, "It is not okay to be wrong or make mistakes." Believing all flaws are fatal, they are tempted to craft the perfect persona by sewing their own fig leaves, a self-made covering of perfection for self-protection. But the good news is that

---

9   Philippians 4:7

10   Genesis 1:31

11   2 Corinthians 5:21

Jesus died on the cross for you—for your flawed self, not your good, improved self. You have been freed *from* criticism—including your own "inner critic" that's always pointing out your shortcomings—and freed *to* make mistakes. After all, you are *perfectly human*. Because God accepts every part of you, you must do the same. The paradox of self-improvement is that you cannot change unless you first accept yourself. Then and only then will your relationships be transformed as you become a grace-giver rather than a grudge-holder, championing progress over perfection.

• **Lie #4: There is only one right way.** The temptation to "be like God"[12] gets expressed in the Improver by taking on the role of judge and seeking to conform others into their ideal image, not God's. Exaggerating their God-given desire for goodness, they begin defining what "should be," convinced they alone know the truth about how the world should work. But through Jesus' death, believers are set free from being terrorized by endless "shoulds." We are now free to please Him with a myriad of choices while also allowing others to walk in freedom. With God's help, you can postpone judgment, expressing your convictions while also leaving room for the perspectives of others.

• **Lie #5: What I *should* do is more important than what I *want*.** Because Improvers are prone to asceticism, or the denial and even demonization of themselves and their desires, God wants you to be more selfish in the best sense of the word, pursuing your giftedness rather than being tied down by what you (or others) think you should do. The defense mechanism of Improvers is called *reaction formation*, which makes them do the opposite of how they feel in order to shield themselves from blame. Ones unconsciously push their "unacceptable" emotions down like a beach ball underwater, presenting themselves in a more socially "acceptable" way. Keeping this mask on indefinitely will only perpetuate the lie that you are not loved for who you really are, but how good you can comply or hold yourself together—and eventually, that ball will burst back above the surface.

• **Lie #6: If something's wrong, it's my responsibility to correct it.** Without God, Improvers carry an unbearable weight on their shoulders to fix everything.

---

12 Genesis 3:5

Everywhere you look, you quickly see things that need improving in yourself, others, or your environment. The deadly sin or vice of the Improver is *resentment*, which kicks in when you think no one else seems to care and that you alone must work overtime to cover for everyone else's complacency. But with God, you will acknowledge that He is ultimately responsible for the world, not you, and be able to slow down, set better work boundaries, spend more time with your loved ones, and prioritize people over projects. Rather than adding responsibilities that God hasn't asked you to take on, you will create more space for the things that truly bring you joy, finding comfort in the fact that practicing self-care is a form of self-improvement.

As you can see, the gospel will challenge your perception of the protagonists and antagonists in your life. In the Improver's merit-based kingdom, good behavior is rewarded, bad behavior is punished, and righteousness is earned. Your heroes become those who work harder than others, don't drop any balls, meet deadlines, and never criticize you (because, after all, you are always right)! Likewise, your villains become those who challenge you to lighten up, go with the flow, take on less responsibilities, accept that your best is good enough, and trust that it doesn't have to be perfect to have peace.[13]

God's kingdom will not be filled with those who proved themselves by being more right than wrong or more good than bad, but rather men and women who received the free gift of righteousness through Christ alone. In this place, judgment is exchanged for discernment, perfection for progress, close-mindedness for curiosity, self-denial for self-expression, and "doing things right" doesn't hold you back from "doing the right things." In this place, structure submits to the Spirit, pleasure is pursued over asceticism, and pursuing your own happiness is not viewed as selfish because God's *glory* and your *good* are one in the same pursuit. In this place, you can let go of your frustration with the way life is and instead rest in the Perfect One who says, "Behold, I am making all things new."[14]

---

13 Typology Podcast, *Part 2: John Mark Comer on Focusing his Attention (Enneagram One) [S03-018]*, podcast audio, November 28, 2019, 4:45, https://www.typologypodcast.com/podcast/2019/28/11/episode03-018/johnmarkcomer-part2.

14 Revelation 21:5

The Invitation

When Jesus Christ, the divine all in all, entered into flawed and limited human history, He started His mission with an invitation: "The time is fulfilled, and the kingdom of God is at hand; repent and believe in the gospel."[15] He explained that to enter the good, eternally renewing life that begins well before the grave, you must do two things: believe the truth and turn from sin. Believing includes acknowledging who God is, who He says we are, and what He has done for us. More than that, to truly believe in a Christlike way is to actively live into those acknowledgments. Turning includes shedding our false worldview, misplaced desires, strong defenses, hide-and-seek strategies, and self-salvation efforts.

If you are ready to begin this incredible 40-day journey and accept God's invitation, then let's go! It will be an enlightening ride of rapid growth in the days to come as you become more self-aware and experience newfound freedom. You will encounter many aha moments as you read profound truths for your type— and maybe even learn something about the people around you. The things you learn about yourself in this book will stick with you for the rest of your life.

Three Types of Improvers

To further explore how Ones can look very different from one another, please check out the "Three Types of Improvers" in the back of this book. These "subtypes" are helpful in understanding the nuances of the Improver and will explain why some truths in this devotional will hit home more than others. These descriptions tend to err on the negative side, but they are meant to help you further uncover the unconscious motivations driving your behavior and may even help you discover why you're often confused with other Enneagram types!

---

15   Mark 1:15

Day 1:

From Chaos to Order

For God is not a God of disorder but of peace ... .

—1 Corinthians 14:33 NIV

IN THE BEGINNING, ALL WAS DARK. THE waters of chaos swirled across the blank canvas of a darkened earth. The Creator stepped in, hovering over the waters. The divine Artist begins painting, sculpting, singing creation into existence. Darkness was divided from light, the waters from the land.[1] With unfathomable knowledge, mathematical formulas spiraled into existence. Then, out of dirt, humanity was sculpted and filled—literally *inspired*—with that creative breath of life. The workmanship was inspected. It was *good*.

> God is a God of systems and predictability and order, and God honors planning.
>
> –Andy Stanley

Man and woman were placed in the garden of Eden as stewards: caretakers, improvers, "to work it and keep it."[2] They joyfully partner with their Creator in ordering this beautiful creation. But then it happened—or rather, it *happens*.

1 Genesis 1:4-9

2 Genesis 2:15

Adam and Eve rebelled, seeking knowledge, control, and power before their time; they *took* with grasping hands what was intended to be joyfully received. By distrusting God's goodness, Adam and Eve began a pattern in which we all continue to participate, snapping the string of harmony, resulting in discord between creation and Creator. Though we were made to live in perfect Eden, sin has made this dream elusive. In relationships, love is often taken or rebuffed, rather than being joyfully received and reflected back. Even worse, no one seems to believe it could be different.

We learn from physics that atoms and their subatomic particles are inherently pure and uncorrupted. However, when they are altered in just the right (or very wrong) way, they can create a nuclear explosion.[3] Similarly, we believe you and I were created perfect at our core—flawless. But because we continue our ancestors' rebellion, the divine design has been altered, and an explosion of grasping corruption has permeated every part of this world.

But the story doesn't end there. The Creator stepped into the narrative as Jesus, reversing the ongoing original sin on the cross receiving both life and death willingly, reflecting only love, and not

> Peace emerges not from our hard work, but our union with Christ.

taking for Himself the "equality with God"[4] He deserved. Now, you and I are invited to partner with Him in this ongoing restoration of the world. We are not saved to wait for heaven, but to partake in reassembling the scattered pieces of light reflecting the Infinite on finite earth.

As an Improver, you reflect God's *perfection* and have a deep longing to experience the purity of our original human state, and to share that perfection with the world.[5] This innate lens allows you to see the brokenness more vividly, leaving you desperate to see the world healed and made whole again. Some Ones reflect this desire by focusing on order in large and small ways: from keeping

---

3   Sandra Maitri, *The Spiritual Dimension of the Enneagram: Nine Faces of the Soul* (New York, NY: Jeremy P. Tarcher/Putnam, a member of Penguin Putnam Inc., 2001), 112-113.

4   Philippians 2:5

5   Marilyn Vancil, *Self to Lose Self to Find: Using the Enneagram to Uncover Your True, God-gifted Self* (New York: Convergent, 2020), 61.

an immaculate home or workplace to leading strongly moral organizations or justice-oriented initiatives.

The Good News for Improvers is that you can experience an all-present, abiding joy despite whatever mess or brokenness you find yourself in. At times, you will experience small glimpses of the "perfection" of Eden, but these moments will be as temporary as the morning dew—moments of refreshment in the work. The state of peace you so long for emerges ultimately not from your hard work, but from pursuing union with Christ. Right now, you can experience a sense of greatness, holy awe, and pure bliss by sitting in the presence of your Perfect Creator.

→ Pray

Father, it brings joy to my heart to know You care more about the chaos in the world and in my life more than anyone—even me. Help me to remember this truth the next time I feel all alone carrying this burden to make things right. I will take my eyes off everything that is wrong in the world and allow You to hold me today as I rest in Your sovereign control over all things.

Day 1 Reflections:

When do you feel most at peace?

Situationally, I feel most at peace when my family is together in the morning sitting around and chatting. All my people together feels like peace. I also feel at peace when I'm caught up on all the things I need to do.

How are you most frustrated with the state of the world right now? Don't hold back.

Generally more frustrated with myself and my lack of patience than I am frustrated at the world. I feel deep sadness for all the pain people are walking around with. If people really knew Jesus we wouldn't hurt each other so much.

What are you hoping to get out of the next 40 days? What would you like to ask God to do?

More of Jesus. Deeper intimacy with God. Lord please heal my heart. Help my inner critic and my inner whimsy become friends. Help me learn to live in the color (grey) and not the black & white.

➜ Respond

Search for, listen to, and meditate on the song "One" from the Sleeping At Last project, Atlas: II.

Day 2:

You and Paul

If anyone else thinks he has reason for confidence in the flesh, I have more: circumcised on the eighth day, of the people of Israel, of the tribe of Benjamin, a Hebrew of Hebrews; as to the law, a Pharisee; as to zeal, a persecutor of the church; as to righteousness under the law, blameless.

—Philippians 3:4b-6

> [The Christian] does not think God will love us because we are good, but that God will make us good because He loves us.
>
> –C.S. Lewis[1]

NO OTHER CHARACTER IN THE BIBLE IN my mind reflects the type One personality more than the apostle Paul—which is why we'll return to his story often. After his conversion, Paul redirected his passion for purity away from the law and ran toward Jesus, who revealed Himself as "the way, and the truth, and the life."[2] Through Jesus, Ones like Paul can finally find the "right

---

1   C. S. Lewis, *The Complete C.S. Lewis Signature Classics* (United Kingdom: HarperCollins, 2007), 59.

2   John 14:6

way," receiving unlimited grace for all their past, present, and future wrongs—especially when their zeal has hurt others.

Because Paul wrote most of the New Testament, we get a front row seat to his journey, watching him leave behind a merit-based, law-centered lifestyle and embrace a grace-based, Christ-centered approach. We witness a man who was angry at others' perceived failings become someone who shed tears over their lapses. To his imperfect church members, he preached the good news that there is no condemnation for those in Christ Jesus.[3]

Paul was often at war with his own heart. His birth and ancestry were impeccable according to Jewish standards, so pride in both his spiritual roots and his own perfection were constant temptations.[4] However, although his old self was considered "blameless" in the eyes of his peers, he chose to tear up his

> We witness a man who was angry at others' perceived failings become someone who shed tears over their lapses.

resume and instead boast about his "rightness" in Christ.[5] Rather than using his accomplishments to show how good he was, he went out of his way to boast about his weaknesses[6]—one of the hardest struggles for a One to do.

"For I know that nothing good dwells in me," said Paul (a harsh statement many Ones resonate with), "that is, in my flesh. For I have the desire to do what is right, but not the ability to carry it out. For I do not do the good I want, but the evil I do not want is what I keep on doing."[7] Though all of us find this to be true, it's the healthy Ones who give the loudest "Amen!" to this vulnerable admission. You have a fear of being bad and the deepest desire to be good, yet find that you don't have what it takes—the self-discipline and willpower to fully and finally reach God's standards for holiness.

---

3 Romans 8:1

4 Philippians 3:4-8

5 Philippians 3:9

6 2 Corinthians 12:9

7 Romans 7:18-19

The Good News for Improvers is that Paul gave zero credit to himself for his growth and maturity. He found serenity, the virtue of a healthy One, by resting in Jesus' continual work in us: "And I am sure of this, that he who began a good work in you will bring it to completion at the day of Jesus Christ."[8] He found solace in the fact that the *goodness* he so desperately wanted is a fruit produced by the Holy Spirit's power rather than his own.

Take the heavy yoke of the law off your shoulders today "for it is God who works in you, both to will and to work for his good pleasure,"[9] and Christ came to offer a lighter burden.[10] One of my favorite lines from Paul is his expression of parental love for his spiritual offspring: "My little children, for whom I am again in the anguish of childbirth until Christ is formed in you!" That is the perfect picture of how God feels about you. Like a pregnant mother, God is in anguish with anticipation and longing for you to grow into your full potential. So relax, what God has started in you, He will bring to completion.

→ Pray

Father, it's incredible to think that You care more about my growth than I do. I've tried so hard to be good and have come up short so often. I'm tired of trying to be good enough on my own. You see the war waging in my soul. Help me rest in the fact that You are working within me as I speak, bearing more beautiful fruit than I ever could've imagined.

---

8   Philippians 1:6

9   Philippians 2:13

10   Matthew 11:30

Day 2 Reflections:

In what ways does Paul's story resonate with your own?

BC Paul was quick to judge others for how fall short they fall. I wonder if Paul was super hard on himself? Right now, I wake up feeling more critical.

How have you seen God mature you in some of the areas where Paul struggled?

I think I grew a lot in self-compassion, but I feel like I'm slipping back into self-criticism mode.

Who in your life are you in anguish over right now? How does knowing that maturity is a fruit of the Spirit rather than a fruit of the flesh change your perspective?

I'm in anguish over myself, my parents. If goodness is a fruit of the spirit, why don't I see it in my dad?
I don't think maturity is a fruit of the spirit, I think goodness is. Maturity comes from growing in all the fruit.

➔ **Respond**

Memorize the opening lines of the Serenity Prayer: "God, grant me the serenity to accept the things I cannot change, the courage to change the things I can, and the wisdom to know the difference."[11]

11   Crosswalk Editorial Staff, "The Serenity Prayer: Full Version, Author, and Bible Meaning," Crosswalk.com, June 17, 2020. https://www.crosswalk.com/faith/prayer/serenity-prayer-applying-3-truths-from-the-bible.html.

Day 3:

You Are Good

For you formed my inward parts; you knitted me together in my mother's womb. I praise you, for I am fearfully and wonderfully made. Wonderful are your works; my soul knows it very well.

—Psalm 139:13-14

ONE OF MY FAVORITE THINGS ABOUT HEALTHY Improvers is how they naturally create and maintain cultures of goodness wherever they go. When people think of Ones, they often picture the most disciplined, hardworking, task-oriented doers they knew. But you are so much more: your passion for ideals, ethics, virtues, and integrity shape whatever room you are in and often result in leadership being given to you.

> The worst feeling in the world is knowing you did the best and it still wasn't good enough.
>
> –Anonymous

We live in a world that has been systemically corrupted with idolatries and ideologies, with the sins of racism and sexism and with political polarization and money-hungry corporate cultures. These toxic environments deplete and drag us down as individuals and communities. But God has commissioned you to bring His purifying light into the spaces you inhabit. He has given you the authority and power to teach and model what a culture of goodness should look like.

Within the body of Christ, Ones function a lot like the digestive system. Wait! Before you shut this book in disgust, read on: your own digestive system helps break down and absorb nutrients from the food and drinks you take in so that your body can grow and develop. It also tells your body what needs to be disposed of. Similarly, you feed and enrich the body of Christ through your instructions and tireless pursuit of what's right and good, helping us discern between teachings, declutter our lives, and cleanse our toxic behaviors. When you use your gifts, the body of Christ is more energized and healthy.

> God has commissioned you to bring His purifying light into the spaces you inhabit.

But before you go out and fulfill your role as a Champion of Good in the world, you first must understand your identity. Before you can help others pursue their truest selves, you must know exactly *who* you are and *whose* you are. Otherwise, you will inevitably end up fighting to heal the world from a place of insecurity or superiority.

In the classic television special *Rudolf the Red-Nosed Reindeer*, we encounter the Island of Misfit Toys. This group of unwanted toys all have a strange quirk about them, such as the "Charlie in the Box," a train with square wheels, and a sinking boat. When Rudolf and his friends (also fellow misfits) stumble upon this island, he learns these toys have been waiting years for suitable owners. Much like the titular character, they have been wondering their whole lives, "When will I ever be good enough? Will I ever fit in?" Do you ever feel like one of these characters—flawed, broken, unqualified for good use?

The Good News for Improvers is that God created the world and saw that it was "very good"[1]—and this includes *you*. You are not some product that must be recalled because of manufacturer defects, for you were woven together in your

---

1 Genesis 1:31

mother's womb by the divine Maker. The King of the island cares for you and sees you as fearfully and wonderfully made. You are *very good*—complete.

Yes, it's true your thoughts and actions fall short in often surprising ways. The apostle Paul, who was also extremely aware of his shortcomings, admits to his young disciple Timothy that he felt like the chief of sinners.[2] Yet, rather than attempting to impress God through self-discipline, self-improvement, or moral comparison, he let go of these old strategies and took hold of his original goodness in Christ.[3]

Remember, your worth is not tied to your goodness (or good efforts) but in your Source. And whatever goodness you feel that you still lack has been fully credited to your account: "For our sake he made him to be sin who knew no sin, so that in him we might become the righteousness of God."[4] In Christ, you have all you need to be worthy of love. Continue to make the world a better place, but never lose sight of the One whose perfection fills every part of you.

→ Pray

Father, forgive me for calling myself bad when You've called me good. The way you designed me is perfect and flawless. Help me see myself through Your gracious eyes rather than through the lens of my inner critic. I will choose today not to dwell on my mistakes, but to think about how perfectly You've covered me with Jesus' righteousness.

---

2 1 Timothy 1:15

3 Philippians 3:8-9

4 2 Corinthians 5:21

Day 3 Reflections:

When has God used you to turn an unhealthy environment or culture into a good one?

Denver gymnastics, Brand RPM

How might your life change, knowing your worth is found in Jesus and not in being a "good boy" or "good girl?"

I think I know that in my head, but it can be hard to believe in my heart. I would have a lot more self-compassion.

What are some ways you can practice self-appreciation more?

Slow down and count the blessings. God has made me uniquely, and there's a lot that's good about me — very good. Asking myself the question: what did you do well today?

→ Respond

To practice self-appreciation, jot down a list of your God-given qualities that you are thankful for.

Lord,
It's hard for me to believe you designed me perfect and flawless because I can see my sin. How my heart is bent toward pride and self-indulgence. I don't want that to be true. Lord I need you. Help me have eyes to see the good. Give me deeper patience in you. I love you Lord.

Day 4:

The Perfect One

So God created man in his own image, in the image of God he created him;

male and female he created them.

—Genesis 1:27

DO YOU REALIZE THAT OTHERS CAN SEE God more clearly through your personality? God created all of us as "mirrors," reflecting different aspects of His heart and character to a broken, hurting world. We are truly the *imago Dei*, translating the infinite, invisible One for a finite, visible world. When walking in the Spirit, you are principled, noble, conscientious, responsible, idealistic, ethical, hardworking, persevering, thorough, pursuing excellence, and working for the good of all.[1]

> We are each of us like a small mirror in which God searches for His reflection.
>
> –St. John Vianney

Pause for a moment and read that list again. You are a remarkable reflection of God's goodness and desire for perfection.

But as you know, it's impossible to reflect those characteristics of God at

---

1   Vancil, *Self to Lose Self to Find*, 69.

all times. The apostle Paul says the mirror was cracked from top to bottom when we exchanged the glory of God for the glory of man.[2] And it's not even a mistake relegated to people of the past; it's something we all do still. When walking in the flesh, all those previous positive attributes turn sour, and you will find yourself being perfectionistic, judgemental, rigid, intolerant, dogmatic, critical of others, overly serious, demanding, uptight, abrasive, and obstinate.[3]

For Ones, the struggle between flesh and Spirit is deeply felt. Riso and Hudson explain that Ones "always feel caught in conflicts: between the perfection of their ideal and their own imperfections; between feeling virtuous and feeling sinful; between their actions and their consciences; between their desire for order and the disorder they see everywhere; between good and evil; between God and the Devil."[4] It ain't easy being a One!

You cannot always reflect God's perfection, but you don't have to—there is One who lived a perfect life for you. He is reliable: as the author of Hebrews says, "Jesus Christ is the same yesterday and today and forever."[5] He is disciplined: though surrounded

> Jesus died on the cross for you—for your flawed self, not your good, improved, crafted self.

constantly with urgent need, Jesus put communion with the Father first: "And rising very early in the morning, while it was still dark, he departed and went out to a desolate place, and there he prayed."[6] He is conscientious: Jesus declared, "For I have come down from heaven, not to do my own will but the will of him who sent me."[7] He always put His duty to right action above His own needs: "Do not think that I have come to abolish the Law or the Prophets; I have not come

---

2 Romans 1:23

3 Vancil, *Self to Lose Self to Find*, 69.

4 Don Riso and Russ Hudson, *Personality Types: Using the Enneagram for Self-Discovery* (HMH Books, 1996), 381.

5 Hebrews 13:8

6 Mark 1:35

7 John 6:38

to abolish them but to fulfill them."[8] And no one had higher standards: "You therefore must be perfect, as your heavenly Father is perfect."[9]

The Good News for Improvers is Jesus died on the cross for you—for your flawed self, not your good, improved, crafted self. You are not worthy because of your good behavior, important causes, attention to detail, or how well you keep your anger in check. You are, right now without any effort, the *imago Dei*. The Holy Spirit is working like a master sculptor to clear away the excess marble and reveal what God sees underneath the image you work so hard to present to others. The Creator and Sustainer of all loves you still, because when He looks in your mirror, He sees the image of His Son reflected back and says, "with you I am well pleased."[10]

→ Pray

Father, thank You for sending Jesus to be my Savior and example, the One who was perfectly reliable, disciplined, conscientious, obedient, and called us to a higher standard. It's frustrating to know I'll never be able to attain His level of perfection in this life, but I take solace in the fact that Your power will rest on me as I boast in my weaknesses and point people to the Perfect One.[11]

Lord,
Help me boast in my weaknesses. There are many, and I really dont want to portray the image that I have it all together, because I really dont. I need you.

---

8   Matthew 5:17

9   Matthew 5:48

10   Mark 1:11

11   2 Corinthians 12:9

Day 4 Reflections:

Which words in the list from the first paragraph reflect the image of God in you?

Responsible, idealistic, hardworking, persevering, pursuing excellence, working for the good of all.

How have you experienced the "flesh and Spirit" struggle described by Riso and Hudson?

Absolutely, 100%. Yes. That's why often rest & relaxation feel so incredibly difficult. There's a constant pull between one side and the other, but I do desire to live more in the middle, the "grey" the color.

What is most inspiring about the way Jesus lived as the "Perfect One?"

That he did it in complete dependence on the Father, constantly taking time away from the noise and the people to just be.

→ Respond

This may be a little uncomfortable, but ask a friend to share how they see these characteristics in you: principled, noble, conscientious, responsible, idealistic, ethical, hardworking, persevering, thorough, pursuing excellence, and working for the good of all.

Day 5:

Perfectly Human

So when the woman saw that the tree was good for food, and that it was a

delight to the eyes, and that the tree was to be desired to make one wise, she

took of its fruit and ate, and she also gave some to her husband who was with

her, and he ate. Then the eyes of both were opened, and they knew that they

were naked. And they sewed fig leaves together and made themselves loincloths.

—Genesis 3:6-7

Being happy doesn't mean that everything is perfect. It means that you've decided to look beyond the imperfections.

−Gerard Way[1]

AFTER EATING THE FORBIDDEN FRUIT, ADAM AND Eve sewed fig leaves to cover the awful feeling of being naked and exposed. While feeling exposed is an unpleasant sensation for everyone, it's particularly unbearable for Improvers, who often say they grew up hearing the message, "It's not okay to make a mistake." Like we've discussed already, Ones believe their flaws are fatal, so they

---

1   Malcolm Bonner, *Be the Parent of Your Child's Dreams: Daily Reflections for Parents in Recovery* (United States: KR Company, Publishers, 2014), 30.

attempt to craft the perfect persona—good, dependable, right, professional, committed, righteous, organized, fair, meticulous, responsible, thorough, and reliable. They avoid (at all costs) looking bad, undependable, wrong, amateur, immoral, careless, unjust, disorganized, impulsive, irresponsible, or sloppy, so they sew their own fig leaves, a self-made image of perfection for the purpose of self-protection.[2]

In doing so, it's almost as if the One is saying, "If I'm perfect, you can't criticize me."[3] Or, put another way, "I will be better than you and rise beyond your capacity to evaluate me: I will show you!"[4] Though Ones know full well they aren't perfect (no one knows better), they feel the temptation to present themselves as such to avoid the pain of criticism, blame, judgment, or feeling like they don't measure up. They will do whatever it takes to ensure that others are not as harsh with them as they are with themselves.

Therefore, Ones can become "feedback fugitives," seeking to avoid being captured by negative feedback. As one Improver shares, "When I find a deficiency in myself or receive

> **Making mistakes is perfectly human.**

criticism, the impact is painful. My inner critic is horrified and humiliated that my failures and imperfections are exposed. Rather than admit my faults, I immediately double down on trying to prove how I am the opposite of these imperfections. Rather than own up, I blame and/or comment on the 'bad' behavior of others so no one will suspect those things go on in me."[5]

What if feedback didn't lead to naked shame and guilt but improved character and health? What if, rather than a personal attack, it became a critical step toward becoming a better person and leader? Make no mistake: your progress tomorrow depends on how well you receive feedback today. The wisdom of Proverbs says

---

2   Scott Loughrige, Clare M. Loughrige, Douglas A. Calhoun, and Adele Ahlberg Calhoun, *Spiritual Rhythms For The Enneagram: A Handbook for Harmony and Transformation* (Downers Grove, IL: InterVarsity Press, 2019), 55.

3   Jerome Peter Wagner, *Nine Lenses on the World: The Enneagram Perspective* (Evanston, IL: NineLens Press, 2010), 167.

4   Claudio Naranjo, *Character and Neurosis: An Integrative View* (Nevada City, CA: Gateways/IDHHB, 1994), 79.

5   Calhoun and Loughrige, *Spiritual Rhythms*, 70.

that a fool runs from life-giving reproof, but the wise person has the humility to listen to it.[6]

Author Brené Brown calls the image of perfectionism a "20-ton shield" that becomes a massive barrier to growth and intimacy with others.[7] Much like the fig leaves our ancestors sewed for themselves, this perfectionism is a heavy burden God has not asked you to carry. Let me ask you an honest question: Do you feel guilty simply for being human? All humans make mistakes, while sins are deliberate choices to do something you know is wrong. I can't overstate enough how much you need to internalize this truth because God accounted for the fact that you would make mistakes when He created you. Making mistakes is *perfectly human*. Besides, if Jesus was willing to die for your sins, how much more will He offer grace for your mistakes?

The Good News for Improvers is that God pursues us whether we sin intentionally or make mistakes unintentionally. No amount of pretending or performing will ever fully obscure your failures before God and others. We know you are human, so don't buy the lie that *perfection is protection*. Put down that 20-ton shield today, relax your defenses, and finally experience the good gift of friendship, connection, and intimacy that God gave you to thrive. When Adam and Eve are naked in shame, God mercifully pursues them and replaces their fragile fig leaves with better garments. He always makes the necessary sacrifice, covering our guilt and shame, just as the prodigal son is met by his father on the road and covered by his father's grace and mercy. Because Jesus, our blameless Savior, was exposed on a humiliating cross and declared guilty for our sins (and mistakes), you can take off your fig leaves and allow yourself to be covered by His love and acceptance.

---

6 Proverbs 15:31

7 Cron and Stabile, *The Road Back to You*, 102.

> ### → Pray
>
> Father, thank You for drawing near to me when I feel paralyzed with guilt. I praise You for sending Jesus to defeat shame on the cross and silence the voice of the Accuser. By the power of the Holy Spirit, help me to release the burden of perfectionism so that I can be fully human and fully loved.

Day 5 Reflections:

When did you start to believe the lie "It's not okay to make a mistake?" What people or life experiences have reinforced that belief?

I want to say gymnastics but I also think my mom had a big impact. It seemed like she never really showed any weakness

Where does a superclean, meticulous, or scrupulous image manifest itself (exaggerated modesty, eating habits, language, body/appearance, etc.)?

Weight, house, eating habits, people's perception of me

How does it feel knowing that making a mistake doesn't make you any less good in God's eyes?

I honestly don't know if I believe that. I know I don't have to perform for Gods love but I also am called to excellence. I can't do it all.

> ### → Respond
>
> Make a mistake on purpose. Don't do a chore or routine you normally do. Put a dish or book on the wrong shelf. Then, smile and remind yourself that all will be well.

Day 6:

The Inner Critic

So to keep me from becoming conceited because of the surpassing greatness

of the revelations, a thorn was given me in the flesh, a messenger of Satan to

harass me, to keep me from becoming conceited.

—2 Corinthians 12:7

THERE WAS ONCE A YOUNG MAN TORMENTED by a red lizard sitting on his shoulder—he hated this vile little beast and its steady stream of negative narration, yet also found he could not imagine life without it. An angel came along and promised to kill it, and the man was happy. Happy, that is, until the angel began glowing with a fiery heat and he realized just how painful this experience would be. Over time, the attached lizard had almost become a part of him, and he wondered if its death would lead to his as well. After some hesitation and promises of pain and loneliness from his evil companion, the lizard was finally killed and a stallion emerged from

> What is this self inside us,
>
> this silent observer,
>
> Severe and speechless critic,
>
> who can terrorize us?
>
> –T. S. Eliot[1]

1   Cron and Stabile, *The Road Back to You*, 98.

where it fell. The newly freed man rode off in joy on this great steed, his greatest shortcoming transforming into his greatest glory.

This lizard, found in C.S. Lewis' *The Great Divorce*, represents an outward manifestation of the man's lust and inner battle to be freed from it, but this insidious creature can also serve as a metaphor for the Improver's inner critic.[2] Much like the apostle Paul describing his "thorn in the flesh" as a "a messenger of Satan to harass me," Lewis's berating lizard is a manifestation of our own self-defeating talk and actions. Sometimes, we are able to be freed from our thorns, while at others (as in Paul's case), they remain as a reminder of our fallibility and limitations.[3]

The One's inner critic, like the man's lizard, shows no mercy, relentlessly reminding you of your shortcomings as well as what you have done and failed to do, could've done better, and on and on. Richard Rohr

> Your inner critic is not the authority in your life—the Holy Spirit is.

says the mind of a One is a courtroom that is "continually in session; they are their own prosecutor, defender, and judge."[4] Ted—a One and a professional carpenter—is proud of his fine craftsmanship and high standards, but admits, "no matter how tough I am on others, I'm always ten times harder on myself. When I actually stop and listen to what I'm saying to myself, I can't believe it. I wouldn't talk like that to my worst enemy!"[5]

When Ones move toward a type Four in stress, they adopt the Four's defense mechanism of introjection. They may "swallow whole" someone else's negative attitudes toward them, allowing perceived negativity from another into their own psyche, and come to deeply believe it themselves. For example, if a parent tells a child "You are dumb"—or if they even *think* the parent feels this way—the child may grow up telling themselves, "I am dumb."

---

2 C. S. Lewis, "One of the most painful meetings we witnessed was between … ," in *The Great Divorce* (New York, NY: HarperCollins, 2009).

3 2 Corinthians 12:7

4 Richard Rohr and Andreas Ebert, *The Enneagram: A Christian Perspective* (New York, NY: The Crossroad Publishing Company, 2001), 50.

5 Don Richard Riso and Russ Hudson, *The Wisdom of the Enneagram: The Complete Guide to Psychological and Spiritual Growth for the Nine Personality Types* (New York, NY: Bantam Books, 1999), 114.

The Good News for Improvers is your inner critic is not the authority in your life—the Holy Spirit is. Your inner critic condemns and punishes, but the Holy Spirit forgives and frees you to experience God's unconditional mercy and love.[6] Just as the lions in John Bunyon's *Pilgrim's Progress* were chained and unable to hurt Christian on his journey, so too is your Accuser chained, unable to afflict harm if you remember you are God's beloved. This is how the apostle Paul quieted the inner-critic in his head, preaching to himself as much as to the Roman church he'd never met: "There is therefore now no condemnation for those who are in Christ Jesus."[7]

Because God accepts you, you must accept yourself. This might sound paradoxical, but the first step to self-improvement is accepting yourself; change is impossible until you do. Start with accepting your past. As Maya Angelou says, "Forgive yourself for not knowing what you didn't know before you learned it." The cross is bigger than all your past, present, and future mistakes. When you believe that, you will become more patient and tolerant of yourself, even allowing some "weeds to grow up with the wheat."[8]

Learn to discern whether the voice in your head is the Accuser's or the Holy Spirit's. Write down the things you hear, especially the cruelest ones, in a journal and then practice Paul's command to "test everything; hold fast what is good."[9] Discuss any repeating messages with someone you trust. If you have the courage to share, they can help you laugh at the ridiculous lies you are believing and help you see yourself accurately. When you see yourself as God sees you, unhealthy criticism will die and what remains will become like a stallion under your control, leading you higher and farther on the journey.

---

6   Beth McCord and Jeff McCord, *Becoming US: Using the Enneagram to Create a Thriving Gospel-Centered Marriage* (Nashville, TN: Morgan James Publishing, 2020).

7   Romans 8:1

8   Wagner, *Nine Lenses on the World*, 185-186.

9   1 Thessalonians 5:21

> **→ Pray**
>
> Father, help me to see myself through Your eyes. Thank You for being a Father and friend who appreciates every part of me. Forgive me for stubbornly refusing to receive Your forgiveness when my sins feel bigger than the cross. Give me ears to listen to the Holy Spirit and mute the voice of the Accuser who has been defeated and rendered powerless over my life.

Day 6 Reflections:

What does your inner critic sound like?

My inner critic can sound like a drill seargant. I think I also don't always recognize the inner critic. Also, it's this constant evaluation of if I'm doing good enough/what I could be doing better.

Do you love who you are? How can you be a better friend to yourself?

More self-compassion. Read "Try softer" again. Less proving myself. I think in my "light" moments, my 4 moments, I really like who I am. It's just continuing to make friends b/w my whimsy & my athlete.

How will you discern between your inner critic and the Holy Spirit?

I think #1 is just noticing the thoughts I'm having, noticing when I'm being critical of myself.

> **→ Respond**
>
> Lord, help me be more aware of my thoughts and my inner critic. I need you.
>
> List the repeating messages you hear about yourself in your head. Discuss them with someone you trust.

Day 7:

Using Your Gifts

I am reminded of your sincere faith, a faith that dwelt first in your

grandmother Lois and your mother Eunice and now, I am sure, dwells in you as

well. For this reason I remind you to fan into flame the gift of God, which is in

you through the laying on of my hands, for God gave us a spirit not of fear but

of power and love and self-control.

—2 Timothy 1:5-7

IF YOU'VE EVER BEEN CAMPING, YOU'RE PROBABLY accustomed to starting fires (or watching your outdoorsy friend do it). Dried leaves or shavings are laid down as kindling, followed by twigs, then increasingly larger sticks, and finally, logs. Once the fire's ablaze, you can then get to the good part—sitting under the stars and soaking up a good conversation. Yet all too soon, the once-roaring flames begin to die. However, rather than starting the process all over again, all you need is to bend down, add fuel, and blow on the glowing embers and they will once again burst into flame.

> I'm silently correcting your grammar.
>
> –An Anonymous One

In his second letter to young Timothy, the apostle Paul challenges his son in the faith not to let his fire die. Timothy is exhorted to "fan" the flame so that his gifts are fully activated, providing light and heat for the church. Paul was concerned that his protégé could—as we all do occasionally—become complacent, allowing his presence and contributions to become cold and lethargic. Timothy's situation is unique in the New Testament as he is the first known "second generation" Christian leader, having been introduced to the gospel by his faithful mother and grandmother.

You might be asking, "*What would it look like for me to 'fan into flame the gift of God'?*" Beatrice Chestnut, in her book *9 Types of Leadership*, describes the One's superpowers. As a One, you provide a roadmap for achieving excellence, creating processes and structures that support productivity and high standards of ethics. You think about all the details, improving everything you put your hands on. You get stuff done on time, with excellence, and without shortcuts. You problem-solve with good questions, providing clarity in the midst of confusion. Your nickname is "Quality Control" and those who know you know that you do things *right*—the *first* time.[1]

good to great

No one tries harder than a One! If you look up "responsible" in the dictionary, others will find your name next to it as a synonym. You are the reason our schools, churches, hospitals, and government buildings stay standing and continue to function. You faithfully and sacrificially give, serve, tithe, and bring your family to church even when you don't feel like it. You never cease to be polite and well-mannered even when you are having a bad day.

> **No one tries harder than a One!**

Thank you for loving us so well. We see your significant, well-intentioned efforts to help us achieve excellence, and know deep down that any harsh words aren't directed at us, but at your own exacting self-standards. You make sure we keep our appointments, follow-through on our health goals, balance the budget, and live out our values and principles. Because of your example, we know what it looks like to live with integrity.

---

1   Beatrice Chestnut, *The 9 Types of Leadership: Mastering the Art of People in the 21st Century Workplace* (Franklin, TN: Post Hill Press, 2017), 59.

The Good News for Improvers is that Christ's love enflames your capacity to be responsible, principled, moral, just, fair, diligent, persevering, and sacrificial. Your natural gifts are part of a grand plan to restore humanity, mirroring Christ's mission from before the dawn of creation: bringing order to chaos and improving a world lacking in virtue and justice. Just as Jesus came and perfectly fulfilled the law, you also help the world fulfill the Great Commandment to love the Lord God with all your heart, soul, mind, and strength and love your neighbor as yourself.[2]

Remember, you didn't start the fire, so you can't put it out! Just as the disciples on the road to Emmaus exclaimed that their hearts were burning after being with Jesus, so too have our hearts been ignited by the Holy Spirit and kept ablaze by walking with Jesus. Our only job is to keep fanning the flame!

→ Pray

Father, I wouldn't be here without You or the friends and family who have invested in me. Thank You for giving me faithful people who have prayed for, taught, disciplined, modeled for, and led me. Help me walk slowly through this world and be a holy and sacrificial presence, pouring out the fire of Your love on a world that's often careless and indifferent.

---

2 Matthew 22:37-39

Day 7 Reflections:

Paul asked Timothy to take inventory of the spiritual deposit made by his mother and grandmother. What spiritual truths and gifts have been passed down to you from your family and/or mentors?

My parents, Katie Peterson + Hannah Chronis, Sophie Bushong, Babette James
Babette - a deep love for God & his Word

Which of the strengths above have been affirmed the most throughout your life?

I'm a leader, I'm hardworking, dependent, responsible

I try really hard and I care a lot

What's one thing you can do to ignite and develop your gifts?

Ask the Lord in prayer and keep spending time in his word.

→ Respond

Identify your strengths and give examples of how you are already using them.

Day 8:

More than One Way

And there came a voice to him: "Rise, Peter; kill and eat." But Peter said, "By no

means, Lord; for I have never eaten anything that is common or unclean." And

the voice came to him again a second time, "What God has made clean, do not

call common."

—Acts 10:13-15

THERE ARE TEN WAYS TO LOAD THE dishwasher, right? I'm fibbing. We both know there is only one way—your way! God's people for centuries had only one way to eat—kosher. That's why the apostle Peter was shaken to the core one day when he went up to pray and fell into a trance, seeing all kinds of unkosher animals, and hearing God say, "Rise, Peter; kill and eat."[1] In the Old Testament, God used food as a visible, outward symbol to distinguish between holy and "common," or that which is impure and unacceptable. But under the new covenant of Christ, God would make the big move to a both-and

> There's more than one
> way to skin a cat.
> —English Proverb

---

1   Acts 10:9-15

diet to accommodate the Gentiles coming into the faith. As you can imagine, Peter really struggled to accept this new reality.

Do you also tend to have a hard time with a both-and approach to life? Do you sometimes feel like the Universe will get off balance if someone doesn't do it your way? After all, you're not opposed to there being a better way in *theory*, you've just not met the person who could prove it! Ones become unhealthy when they are convinced they alone know the truth about how the world should work. Like Peter, who went so far as to *disagree with God* on the dietary issue, unhealthy Ones hold onto their opinion like a dog with a bone that cannot be wrestled from him.[2]

Healthy Ones are a blessing, serving as moral compasses helping to constrain evil in the world. You pay close attention to your conscience and this motivates you to do what is right.[3] What's equally praiseworthy is that you strive to base all of your opinions not on your own subjective reality, but on objective, timeless truths and principles.

> Express your convictions with the world, but don't forget to leave room for others' perspectives.

However, this strength of yours can go south quickly if you hold the opinions (that you attach to these principles) with the same moral weight. For example, because "God is love" is a timeless truth, and red is the color symbolizing love, a One might share their "conviction" that the church *should* be painted red. This is a silly example but you get the point: opinions can move to convictions quickly.

Pastor and theologian Andrew Wilson proposes that biblical truth can be divided into three categories of certainty: blood, ink, and pencil. Blood issues are matters of conviction that we would die for. Ink issues are things we believe in practice, feel we must have to thrive, and will defend with some conviction but may change our mind about later on. Finally, pencil issues are opinions that can be explained and articulated but that might be erased and replaced after a time.[4]

---

2   Maitri, *The Spiritual Dimension of the Enneagram*, 125.

3   Riso and Hudson, *Personality Types*, 387.

4   Andrew Wilson, "Pencil, Ink and Blood," Think Theology, September 10, 2012, https://thinktheology.co.uk/blog/article/pencil-ink-and-blood.

The path of growth for you will include doing the hard work of distinguishing between ink, blood, and pencil issues (theological and otherwise), and then choosing not to hold them all with equal weight. This will allow you to be both close-handed, standing up for the things that actually matter, and graciously open-handed with things that don't matter as much. Over the years, I regret putting far too much time and energy into debating the non-essentials.

The Good News for Improvers is you don't have to fight to be right because you are already good. Somewhere down the line you might have gotten the impression that to be *loved* you have to be *good*, and to be *good* you have to be *right*.[5] Because you have been declared righteous through Jesus Christ, you can't make yourself more right in God's eyes than you already are.[6] You can relax your defenses like Peter and allow God to show you a vision of a more colorful world. When Peter finally let go of his black-and-white thinking, his judgment toward the Gentiles subsided, his gospel witness toward them accelerated, and he enjoyed a new and exciting fellowship with these brothers and sisters in Christ. Therefore, continue to express your convictions with the world, but don't forget to leave room for others' perspectives. Your relationships depend on it. I heard that a counselor once asked a One, "Would you rather be right or be happy?"

→ Pray

Father, thank You for giving me the desire to live with a good conscience every day. Help me live out my convictions with boldness and my opinions with gentleness. This is extremely difficult, but I know Your Holy Spirit will guide me with truth and grace. Give me an open-hearted curiosity to eagerly explore new perspectives and ways of doing things.

---

5   Riso and Hudson, *The Wisdom of the Enneagram*, 110.

6   Romans 5:1

Day 8 Reflections:

How does the desire to be right come out in your life?

Often times this comes out in my feelings/emotions - I want to be sure I'm "feeling" the "right way" about a situation. It feels bad if my emotions/feelings/thoughts are perceived as too "many" much in comparison to the situation. I feel like I often know the right way to be.

What are your blood, ink, and pencil beliefs?

Blood: love God + love others

Where in your life (or theology) do you need to learn to be more open-handed?

With myself. I need to learn that its ok to be messy. It's ok to have emotions & opinions.

→ Respond

To stretch yourself and broaden your perspective, choose a position that is the opposite of your usual view and try to argue it convincingly with someone else.[7]

---

7   Riso and Hudson, *The Wisdom of the Enneagram*, 111.

Day 9:

Don't Should on Others

But if someone says to you, "This has been offered in sacrifice," then do not eat

it, for the sake of the one who informed you, and for the sake of conscience—I

do not mean your conscience, but his. For why should my liberty be determined

by someone else's conscience? If I partake with thankfulness, why am I

denounced because of that for which I give thanks?

—1 Corinthians 10:28-30

PHILOSOPHERS LOVE DEBATING "NO WIN" MORAL DILEMMAS, such as the infamous trolley problem, or whether one

> He who can no longer
> listen to his brother
> will soon be no longer
> listening to God either.
>
> –Dietrich Bonhoeffer[1]

should lie to the Nazis in order to save a Jew in hiding. Theological giants of the past, such as Augustine and Aquinas, argued that lying is never permissible under any circumstance, even if others must die.[2] While I don't hold that view, I can see the tension: giving someone the freedom not to tell the truth

---

1 Stephen J. Nichols, *Bonhoeffer on the Christian Life: From the Cross, for the World* (Wheaton, IL: Crossway, 2013), 72.

2 David Livingstone Smith, "The Morality of Lying," Encyclopedia Britannica (Encyclopedia Britannica, Inc.), accessed April 1, 2022, https://www.britannica.com/topic/lying/The-morality-of-lying.

could undermine the moral fabric of society. As an Improver, you know the feeling that under all freedom is a treacherously slippery slope.

Oftentimes, there is not a clear-cut good/evil option on the table to choose from. In fact, much of life is deciding between two competing *good* values—like being truthful versus saving a life. We are all called to use wisdom in every context to decide which competing value will lead to the highest good.

It will help you as a One to realize that others with opposing "bad" views might actually be defending another good value! Context matters a great deal and, though you may not recognize it, even your seemingly easy decisions between "right" and "wrong" do not take place in a vacuum. Often, you will find yourself trying to fit *your* square peg of a value into the round hole of someone else's context. Slow down, take a breath, and seek to learn more about where others are coming from.

When convinced they are the only ones being logical, unhealthy Ones have been known to get on a soapbox, taking on a sermonizing speaking style. Helen Palmer illustrates Improvers' syllogistic thinking, as they unconsciously turn "I wants" into "You shoulds": for example, "if a One likes to cycle, then suddenly bicycles are the right way to get around town, and other means of transportation are wrong by definition. Cars pollute the atmosphere, cars are dangerous, cars are bad. Cycling is clean, healthful, and good. Once they establish cycling as the one right way, Ones will cycle to work and make it clear to anyone they encounter that the world would be a better place if they changed."[3]

> Give others freedom to make their own choices guided by their own consciences.

From the viewpoint of the One, it's an *act of love* to make suggestions! Though others may receive your "shoulds" in the wrong way sometimes, I know you are only trying to help us make positive changes and be the best that we can be. The more I understand this dynamic, the more appreciative and open-hearted I've become toward the Ones in my life.

---

3   Helen Palmer, *The Enneagram in Love and Work: Understanding Your Intimate and Business Relationships* (New York, NY: HarperOne, 2010), 53.

Don't stop teaching and improving our lives; it's making a real difference in the world. Just make sure to give others freedom to make their own choices guided by their own consciences. Releasing others into the Christ-guaranteed freedom of their own contexts offers liberty for both them *and* you. The apostle Paul taught that our Spirit-guided conscience, not legalism, shows us the boundary markers of sin. For a first-century Jew, if eating food sacrificed to idols went against his or her conscience, it was a sin. That's why if you were to dine with them, Paul says, you should restrict your freedom out of love for them. However, Paul continues, that person can't turn around and say, "*You* should never eat food sacrificed to idols too" because that would be taking away your freedom.

To respect the freedom of others and not cross a boundary, practice saying things less conclusively, like "I might not see the full picture," or "I could be wrong here." This will open yourself up to others' views and motivate them to want to listen to your perspective more.[4] You can also remove some of your moral intensity by substituting words like "should, ought, right, and wrong," for words like "might, could, and possible."[5]

The Good News for Improvers is that with God's help, you can accept the values-based and conscience-led choices others make without feeling the need to overcorrect them. The Pharisees tyrannized others with their "shoulds" by developing a system of 613 laws, producing a joyless brand of religion by the time Jesus came.[6] But through His death, believers are now set free from being terrorized by endless "shoulds." The new covenant has been written on our hearts, and through the Holy Spirit, we are now free to please Him with a myriad of choices; allowing others to walk in the freedom Christ purchased for them is an act of trust in that same Spirit who resides in you.[7]

---

4   Calhoun and Loughrige, *Spiritual Rhythms*, 69.

5   Ginger Lapid-Bogda, *Bringing Out the Best in Everyone You Coach: Use the Enneagram System for Exceptional Results* (United Kingdom: McGraw-Hill Education, 2009).

6   J. Stowell, "Pharisaic Laws," Bible.org, February 2, 2009, https://bible.org/illustration/pharisaic-laws.

7   Hebrews 8:8

> **→ Pray**
>
> Father, I get overwhelmed at times because there is so much in this world that needs correcting. I feel responsible before You to do everything I can to help others to honor You with their attitudes and actions. Remind me today that I'm not responsible for it all and must leave room for the Spirit to work. Help me discern what is mine and not mine to fix.

Day 9 Reflections:

When has someone encroached on your freedom? How did it make you feel?

_____

_____

_____

_____

How have you gotten on a "soapbox" in the past? What opinions of yours felt like absolute truths?

Healthy eating
_____

_____

_____

What do you discern is and isn't yours to fix in the lives of others?

I'm still working on this, but "power, control, responsibility" feels like a tool that helps me grasp whats mine and what is not mine to fix.

> **→ Respond**
>
> Try to catch yourself in the act today saying "should, ought, right, or wrong" and instead use "might, could, or possible."

Day 10:

Slow Down

For in six days the LORD made heaven and earth, the sea, and all that is in them, and rested on the seventh day. Therefore the LORD blessed the Sabbath day and made it holy.

—Exodus 20:11

ONE AFTERNOON I ENDED UP ON THE shoulder of the interstate in my wife's Geo Prizm. Minutes before, the engine had begun making clunking noises and soon, the poor car sputtered its last breath as I pulled off the road, suddenly remembering the oil change I'd been "meaning" to do. Just as I figured my wife's car could keep going without an oil change, I thought I could keep going—keep achieving—without rest. But I was wrong. I kept reminding myself to take a break like I remembered to take the car into the shop: something always to be done later.

> **Most of the things we need to be most fully alive never come from pushing. They grow in rest.**
>
> –Mark Buchanan[1]

---

1   Mark Buchanan, *The Holy Wild: Trusting in the Character of God* (United Kingdom: Crown Publishing Group, 2009), 222.

Ones (and Threes, like me) prefer not to slow down. There's no difference, really, between a Tuesday, Saturday, or a Sunday if there's work to be done. Rest, silence, solitude, or even leisure activities can become obstacles, which is why our phones are never far away. It's nearly impossible to log out, disconnect, and shut down.

Free time can actually make a One *more* anxious, so you push yourself beyond your limits of endurance due to the neverending checklist of "shoulds." Unhealthy Ones have a "bit and bridle in their mouth, pulling their obligations, and often experience tautness in their jaws resulting from their resentment and striving."[2] As Riso and Hudson point out, "there are few vacations from their obligations."[3]

When Ones slow down and rest, they almost become a different person—humorously similar to the famous description of mullets: "business in the front, party in the back." One Executive Pastor I know has received the nickname "Nick at Nite" from his co-workers because of the playful version of himself that comes out after work hours. Another friend of mine who is a school teacher has received the nickname "Summer Kyle" from his students because of the spontaneous side that comes out during summer break.

> When Ones slow down and rest, they almost become a different person.

Helen Palmer explains the reason behind this phenomenon: "Ones change radically when they're freed from responsibility." She continues, "Like a kid whose homework is done, they can go out and play. … A One away from home likes to play. Relationships flourish with scheduled vacations, in a way that they never could in a familiar setting. There's simply too much to do at home."[4]

Watch for the "Check Engine" light to come on in your life. When you become responsible for too many things and ignore the rhythms of life or the calls of your loved ones, burn out or physical and mental breakdowns are not far behind. Don't let your "shoulds" interfere with your enjoyment of life and let your

---

2   Wagner, *Nine Lenses on the World*, 181.

3   Riso and Hudson, *Personality Types*, 392.

4   Palmer, *The Enneagram in Love and Work*, 44.

responsibilities replace intimacy. After all, while we faithfully hope for rest in the hereafter, Christ came to bring it to us first in the here-and-now.

God knew what He was doing when He gave the command to rest, initiating the cycle in the act of creation itself. Life is intended to have these consistent sequences: we work and then we rest and trust that the world will keep spinning even if we stop. This is not easy; our society idolizes overwork. Most will look down on you if you are caught stealing, but stealing moments away from your God-given rest is a sign of work ethic and commitment.

The Good News for Improvers is that Jesus has redeemed us from being human *doings*, just as God redeemed the Israelites from being slaves in Egypt. The taskmaster's commands of "shoulds" have been silenced, replaced with the voice that says, "Come to me, all who labor and are heavy laden, and I will give you rest."[5] In the presence of Him whose load is easy and whose burden is light, we are freed from being overly fixated on tasks, new projects, goals, and what's next. Finally, we are free to rest—to be human *beings*.

Without rest or taking a vacation, you can make very efficient use of your *chronos* (chronological) time, but be totally missing out on your *kairos* (divine moments) time that God spontaneously brings into your life. So remember, the most significant thing God might have you do today may not be on your planner.

→ Pray

Father, You are all-powerful, all-knowing, and all-present. You never sleep or slumber. Yet You taught through example the need for a rhythm in life and for rest. Forgive me for forgetting that I am in Your image, an image in need of the Sabbath rest You've created for me. Thank You for sending Jesus to set me free from being a slave so that I might enjoy Your rest.

---

5   Matthew 11:28

Day 10 Reflections:

When was the last time you took extended rest or a vacation? How did others experience you differently? How did it make you feel to see others loosen up around you?

I like myself best when I'm "vacation claire." I think people like me better too - I feel more relaxed and lighter.

What is your biggest challenge to taking time off (feeling lazy, unproductive, losing control, God's wrath, etc.)?

It feels like I can't do it while in Charlotte, there's too many things that need to get done. Help me, Lord.

How would more rest improve your relationships?

Not feeling so overwhelmed that I can't call people back or respond to texts.

→ **Respond**

Going to portugal next week!

Plan your next vacation.

Day 11:

Self-Care

I perceived that there is nothing better for them than to be joyful and to do good

as long as they live; also that everyone should eat and drink and take pleasure

in all his toil—this is God's gift to man.

—Ecclesiastes 3:12-13

IMAGINE WALKING INTO YOUR FAVORITE LOCAL SANDWICH shop and coming to the realization that it's a one-woman operation. She's the owner, cashier, sandwich maker, and janitor all in one. Though she's always making sandwiches for her growing number of customers, she never seems to eat. As months of lunch breaks go by, you notice she's beginning to look unhealthy. Once energetic, she now looks pale and exhausted. Though the shop has an abundance of food, she is forgetting to feed herself.[1]

> Sometimes you don't realize you're actually drowning when you're trying to be everyone else's anchor.
>
> –Unknown

---

1 Illustration adapted from Tim Ellmore, "The Starving Baker for Teachers," Growing Leaders, September 9, 2011, https://growingleaders.com/blog/the-starving-baker-for-teachers/.

Similarly, Improvers have a way of satisfying others while starving themselves. But Jesus came so that "your joy may be full"[2] and this happens through abiding, not striving. As the author of Ecclesiastes learned, slowing down to eat, drink, and feel pleasure is God's gift to us. He says there is nothing better than to *be joyful and do good.* Sounds like the perfect One motto to me!

Your lifelong path of growth will include ignoring the call of duty at times and instead, choosing to play and do something that brings you pleasure, even if it doesn't feel "worthwhile." Ones have shared that they feel guilty just watching a television show or movie unless it "improves" them in some way, but this mindset has come to be understood more and more as potentially destructive. Therefore, you must mute the inner critic's voice telling you it's wrong or wasteful to do something for yourself and instead remind yourself of this truth: self-care *is* self-improvement; you can't help make the world whole until you are.

On the Enneagram, a One moves to the high side of Seven when healthy and secure. When this move happens, Ones lighten up, become more spontaneous, and the seemingly

> Self-care is self-improvement.

"inappropriate" childlike playfulness they've suppressed comes out. When you tap into that side of you, you can be one of the most playful types on the Enneagram. The wife of a One friend of mine recently caught him busting out his old high school show choir choreography. He typically wears a serious demeanor as a successful CFO, but that day, he was dancing for his four-month-old, who stared up at him in wide-eyed amazement from her spot on the floor. You should tap into that free-spirited side of you today—it's perfectly allowed.

Make a list of the things that give you joy: schedule some "planned fun"—and choose not to feel guilty for it; allocate thirty minutes a day to doing something that gives you life; spend time with people who make you laugh and help you not to take yourself too seriously. Make it a habit to use your natural humor to lighten up whatever room you are in—whether at home or in a business meeting.

Because you are in the body triad, anger is your primary emotion and you tend to suppress it, holding it within your body. Getting regular massages may release

---

2 John 15:11

that pent-up tension. Exerting yourself physically in some way helps too. This could be going to the gym, running, boxing, martial arts, or even dancing—anything that gives you permission to express yourself and counterbalance your serious side. Going outdoors can also be a life-giving practice for Ones. A walk or hike will relax your whole being and stir your heart because in the outdoors there is nothing for you to improve. In nature, you can just *be* in God's perfect creation.

The Good News for Improvers is you can let go of the pressure to always be "the adult" and embrace childlike joy. The joyful bliss you are longing for is not at the end of a project, but in the presence of God—who, I have to remind you, is *everywhere*.[3] King David sang, "In your presence there is fullness of joy; at your right hand are pleasures forevermore."[4] This is the most important thing to remember: *Self-care* without *soul-care* is *self-ish* care. True, holistic self-care includes not only resting from enterprise and expectation, but bathing our souls in the One who makes us whole. The activities that bring this wholeness are as varied as the people who do them, but they will in some measure follow the example of Jesus' twin pursuits of prayer and community.

→ Pray

Father, thank You for sending Your Son Jesus to die for my sins and restore my joy. It was "for the joy"[5] that He labored and endured. Let that be my end goal as well. Help me to slow down and take pleasure in the gifts You've given me. I'm letting go of the need to be in control and perfect the world today so that I can put on childlike joy.

---

3   Psalm 139:7-12

4   Psalm 16:11

5   Hebrews 12:2

Day 11 Reflections:

Why do you feel guilty for being selfish with your time?

If I'm being selfish with my time and not getting everything done I feel like I'm letting people down or being lazy.

What things in life bring you the most joy?

singing in the car with Tucker
slow mornings with my family
playing pickleball with friends
sitting around a table with friends/family

How does your schedule need to change for you to prioritize self-care?

It's such a hard balance b/c for me oftentimes rest/play happens best with other people, so you have to plan. But then that somehow makes my schedule feel too full.

→ Respond

Do something life-giving today for pure enjoyment rather than a desired outcome.

Day 12:
Improving Relationships

Love is patient and kind; love does not envy or boast; it is not arrogant or rude.

It does not insist on its own way; it is not irritable or resentful; it does not

rejoice at wrongdoing, but rejoices with the truth. Love bears all things, believes

all things, hopes all things, endures all things.

—1 Corinthians 13:4-7

THE FIRST TIME WE SIT BEHIND THE wheel of a car, we discover that what we *can't* see may hurt us. The safest way to drive is practicing constant awareness, minding our vehicle's blind spots and attending to the flow and rhythm of traffic. The same is true when navigating relationships: our failure to see the needs of those with whom we live and work can lead to unintentional pain for all. There is a rhythm and a flow—a giving and receiving—in relationships that must be minded, so today, we are going to take a hard but necessary look at some of the blind spots that come with being a One.

> You don't love someone because they're perfect, you love them in spite of the fact that they're not.
>
> –Jodi Picoult[1]

---

1   Jodi Picoult, *My Sister's Keeper - Movie Tie-In: A Novel* (United States: Washington Square Press, 2009), 384.

In the apostle Paul's classic chapter on love in 1 Corinthians, we learn about many of these blind spots. For instance, true, Christlike love does not seek to get its own way: relationships suffer when one party falls into black-and-white thinking and believes their way is the only possible right way. Love is not arrogant: this means having the humility to accept criticism when it comes our way without getting defensive. Love is not rude: seeking opportunities to be kind and gentle rather than nitpicky or scolding toward others when they make mistakes; letting most go (because, let's be honest, you see *all* of the mistakes!) and choosing carefully which you will respond to with an eye toward accepting instruction. Love is not irritable: not stuffing our anger and letting it come out sideways through moodiness or withdrawing. Nor is love resentful: it doesn't hold our loved ones to strict, unspoken standards, then expressing offense or exasperation when they inevitably fail.[2]

Now pause. Take a breath. Every single one of us have blind spots and yours aren't worse than any others.

What's equally important for you to be aware of are your relational *strengths*. For instance, you show us how love bears all things by your unswerving loyalty and commitment. Through your disciplined work on relationships, we see how love endures all things. You are always quick to see what is happening right in front

> The better friend you are to yourself, the better of a friend you'll be to others.

of you and serve sacrificially. You are kind, honest, and thoughtful, putting an enormous amount of time and thought behind every response and action you take. This leads to your comforting calm demeanor in the face of conflict: you may be boiling under the surface, but you keep your cool and seek resolution.[3]

Looking ahead, the most important thing you can do in improving your relationships is to be kind to yourself. As you come to accept your identity as a beloved child of God, you can quiet the berating inner-voice that causes your self-frustration, which is inevitably projected onto others. The better friend you are to yourself, the better friend you'll be to others. Another proactive thing you

---

2   1 Corinthians 13:4-5

3   Palmer, *The Enneagram in Love and Work*, 29.

can do is take more time to process and share your emotions, anger and all. Do not be afraid of the unknown emotions bubbling within: tell your loved ones, "I want you to know I'm present with you, and I'm feeling something, but I'm just not sure what yet,"[4] and they will quite often return warmth, intimacy, and trust. Remember, we want the real you, not the polished version.

The Good News for Improvers is that in the light of Jesus' life of sacrificial love, we can see our blind spots and strengths more clearly. Through Jesus, the multi-faceted love of the Triune Godhead described in 1 Corinthians 13 has been made visible to us in flesh and bone. His life has given us a path that we are to follow. Just as a diverse spectrum of bright colors shine through a crystal prism, so too do the patience, kindness, truth, and enduring love of the Father shine through the Son with magnificent glory, and we ourselves are called to continue reflecting that light. If you have seen and tasted this radiant love, you ought to go and love others in the same way today.

→ Pray

Father, I know what love is because You first loved me. When it comes to loving others, I fall incredibly short of Your standard. But Your love is perfect toward me even though I am imperfect. Through the Holy Spirit's power, help me to comprehend the magnitude of Your love so I can cover my imperfections (and others') with Your grace and kindness.

---

4   Ibid, 30.

Day 12 Reflections:

Which aspect of Paul's definition of love do you struggle with the most?

I can definitely be irritable and moody, I can withdraw and just be harsh. Especially to my Mom, and I am not proud of that.

What relational strength of yours are you most proud of and why?

My loyalty to others - when I find my people I love them deeply and will do almost anything for them.

Where in your life do you feel guilt or regret? Open your hands and receive God's abundant grace today.

I feel guilt over my relationships with my parents- like it's on me to figure out how to go back to the way things were.

→ Respond

Identify a person you are struggling to love. List the unspoken expectations you have for them. Are they realistic? Have you communicated these yet? Try reevaluating your expectations and re-engage with more patience.

Day 13:

Good Anger

Be angry and do not sin.

—Ephesians 4:26a

HAVE YOU EVER SHOUTED, "THAT'S NOT FAIR!"? Whether you said this as a child who received fewer pieces of pizza than your sibling, or more recently, while taking a stand in the workplace or public sphere, the source is the same: righteous anger. Though expressing anger is frowned upon in most church circles, it's not always sinful. God did not say anger is *never* allowed, but rather, "Be angry and do not sin."[1] Righteous anger is different from unrighteous anger in two important ways: first, righteous anger is *God-centered*—triggered by the same things that anger God, such as injustice and hypocrisy. Second, righteous anger is *controlled*—expressed in planned, often prophetic ways.

> He who is not angry when there is just cause for anger is immoral.
>
> –Thomas Aquinas

Righteous anger does not seek to destroy but is an expression of love meant to move us from the often unjust status quo, through disorientation, and into a

---

1 Ephesians 4:26

new, more God-honoring order. We see throughout the Scriptures how righteous indignation leads to good action—anger toward sin moved God to purify His people and the prophets to take a stand in the face of injustice. In church history, we see leaders like Martin Luther break out in rage over the purchase of indulgences for salvation. His righteous anger toward practices within his own church sparked a worldwide reformation.

Like Luther, when Ones transmute their anger into good energy, they leave behind the comforts of the world and bravely pursue a higher calling. As Riso and Hudson teach, "More than those of any other personality type, healthy Ones willingly put themselves on the line for their moral beliefs and would rather suffer injustice themselves than act unjustly toward anyone else."[2] John the Baptist is a striking example, suffering injustice at the hands of King Herod for taking a moral stand against him—a stand which would find him imprisoned and ultimately beheaded.[3]

Whether or not John is an Eight like some Enneagram teachers have suggested, Improvers will find much in his life to be admired. His entire ministry was centered on baptizing others, a ritual representing

> Righteous anger does not seek to destroy but is an expression of love.

moral cleansing and a change of heart. John became an example to others of righteous living, but did not point to himself as the perfect standard. Rather, like a truly healthy One, John released his ego and said, "He must increase, but I must decrease."[4] Being a teacher, he answered the crowd's question, "What then shall we do?"[5] with moral principles like sharing their food and clothes with the needy and not extorting money from others. He taught them how to live just and fair lives.

The Good News for Improvers is that you have permission to be righteously angry. Though Jesus storming the temple with His makeshift whip of cords is often portrayed as Him losing His temper, a better reading reveals this as

2   Riso and Hudson, *Personality Types*, 389.

3   Mark 6:18b

4   John 3:30

5   Luke 3:10

a planned act to make a prophetic point. Out of love for those wishing to be near God, Jesus turned His inner anger into righteous action by driving out the money-hungry opportunists that were keeping people distant from Him.

You too, like John, have been given the high calling of making straight paths, setting crooked things right, and bearing witness to the truth that all may believe through Jesus.[6] You might see yourself as a rational being, making logical decisions with your mind, but deep down you are an activist led by a heart that burns for the Lord.

Continue to find your passion as you discover what angers the heart of God, and then channel it for constructive purposes. Think about this: Where would the world be without the likes of Frederick Doulgass and Sojourner Truth, or Susan B. Anthony and William Wilberforce—those who passionately sought to right the wrongs of their times and places? As you reflect on the brave stories of these saints and others, let these words from the prophet Isaiah be your benediction today: "Learn to do right; seek justice. Defend the oppressed. Take up the cause of the fatherless; plead the case of the widow."[7]

→ Pray

Father, break my heart for what breaks Yours. Though I despise being an angry person, help me get in touch with my good anger and use it in a prophetic way. Help me pay attention to the impulses my body feels when I see sin and injustice around me. With courage from the Spirit, help me to act on those impulses rather than suppress them.

---

6   John 1:7

7   Isaiah 1:17 NIV

Day 13 Reflections:

Do you think of anger as an asset? Why or why not?

No, I often think of anger as a "bad" feeling, one that I shouldn't feel or express.

Which of these injustices makes you most angry and why: <u>abuse</u>, violence, illness, betrayal, <u>addiction</u>, poverty, racism, or <u>abandonment</u>? What else would you add to this list?

I think these make me the most angry because of my personal experience with them.

How can you channel that anger for constructive purposes?

Honestly, I don't know and that's why it's so hard to figure out what to do about my dad. I don't know how to appropriately display my anger.

→ Respond

Keep an anger journal to begin tracking your passions under the surface that could be converted into right action.

Day 14:

Angry Virtue

Then Jesus said to him, "Put your sword back into its place. For all who take the sword will perish by the sword."

—Matthew 26:52

NASRUDDIN STOOD ON THE DECK OF THE ship, speaking with the famous scholar. Every time he spoke, the scholar mocked him: "I've never heard such atrocious language. Didn't you study grammar in school?" Nasruddin shook his head. "Well," said the scholar, "I'd say you've wasted your life." During their voyage, a great storm arose and it became clear all was lost. "Abandon ship!" shouted the captain. Nasruddin turned to the terrified scholar and asked, "Didn't you study swimming in school?" but the man shook his head. "Well," said Nasruddin, "I'd say you've wasted your life." Then he jumped into the water and swam safely to shore.[2]

> Of all bad men, religious bad men are the worst.
>
> —C.S. Lewis[1]

The scholar is a striking image of those who "major in the minors" like the Pharisees whom Jesus told were "straining

---

1   C.S. Lewis, *Reflections on the Psalms* (Orlando, FL: Harcourt Inc., 1958), 32.

2   Laura Gibbs, "Stories and Storytelling Ideas: Nasruddin's Grammar" Tiny Tales Teaching Guide, July 26, 2020, https://tinytalesguide.pressbooks.com/chapter/chapter-1/.

out a gnat and swallowing a camel."[3] This is a personally soothing story, since it's nice to see the pedants and grammarian "scholars" among us—who love to point out the smallest mistakes—find out they've literally missed the boat. Sixteenth century Spanish priest St. John of the Cross wrote about the kind of spiritual people who "become irritated at the sins of others, and keep watch on those others with a sort of uneasy zeal. At times the impulse comes to them to reprove them angrily, and occasionally they go so far as to indulge it and set themselves up as masters of virtue. All this is contrary to spiritual meekness."[4]

Enneagram teacher Claudio Naranjo referenced these words from John to describe unhealthy Improvers, calling their excessive indignation "angry virtue."[5] We also see this in the apostle Paul's life who, prior to his

> We can lose our goodness in trying to prove our rightness.

conversion, was a moral crusader protecting what he saw as the purity of his people. As a "Pharisee of Pharisees," it was his zeal for the law that led him to be a persecutor of the church.[6] His anger was so "righteous" it gave his conscience the justification it needed to stone to death Christians like Stephen who were on the "wrong" side.[7]

We witness the same thing happen through the Crusades in the Middle Ages, to the "Doctrine of Discovery" in the fifteenthth century, when public decrees were issued by the Pope commissioning the brutal conquest of "savages" deemed "enemies of Christ" in Africa and the Americas—a doctrine with a straight line to the genocide of Native Americans, slavery, and many of our modern global conflicts throughout the world. This subjugation of all non-Christian lands was supposedly rooted in the virtue of spreading the "right religion."[8]

So, what does this have to do with you?

---

3   Matthew 23:24

4   Saint John of the Cross, *Dark Night of the Soul* (New Kensington, PA: Whitaker House, 2017), 14.

5   Naranjo, *Character and Neurosis*, 64.

6   Philippians 3:6

7   Acts 22:20

8   "The Doctrine of Discovery, 1493," The Gilder Lehrman Institute of American History, accessed February 15, 2022, https://www.gilderlehrman.org/history-resources/spotlight-primary-source/doctrine-discovery-1493.

My guess is that, like me, you are no modern-day crusader. But these stories show the lengths to which humans will go if we believe, like the Bob Dylan song says, we have "God on our side." Like Peter, any of us have the potential to pick up our sword and lash out at others if we believe we're on the "right team."[9] But the strategy of cutting others down "in Jesus' name" will be the end of us—it makes us "good in the worst sense of the word" as Mark Twain put it.[10]

Ask yourself, "How far am I willing to go when I *know* I'm right?" A pastor I knew once said to another pastor (one of those who was legitimately smarter than everyone else ... and knew it), "It's not that you are wrong. I know you're right. But you're being a jerk." That has been lodged in my memory as a reminder that we can lose our goodness in trying to prove our rightness.

The Good News for Improvers is that Jesus demonstrates how to make the world moral without responding immorally. He came into the world not to give wrath but to take it upon Himself. Like we talked about yesterday, good anger, expressed "by the meekness and gentleness of Christ"[11] is a reflection of God's heart and one's moral character. This is all easier said than done, but don't worry; by the power of the Holy Spirit, you *will* be able to steward your anger in the right time, in the right way, and for the right purposes.

→ Pray

Father, I am in awe of You for being slow to anger although You feel the injustices of the world on a cosmic scale. Thank You for enduring wrath on the cross and giving me what I don't deserve—grace upon grace. I beg You today to give me the Spirit's discernment in helping me know when to offer correction and when to receive this imperfect world with open, loving arms.

---

9   Matthew 26:52

10   Calhoun and Loughrige, *Spiritual Rhythms*, 57.

11   2 Corinthians 10:1

Day 14 Reflections:

When was the last time you knew you were right (but unkind) in a conversation?

_____

_____

_____

_____

How did Jesus accomplish so much good without wielding a sword against the Romans (or us!)?

_____

_____

_____

_____

Who can you learn from who is fighting for good in constructive ways?

_____

_____

_____

_____

→ Respond

When you interact with someone who is outright wrong or immoral, remind yourself you can lead a horse to water, but you can't make it drink. As Jesus did, entrust that person to the Father who "judges justly"[12] and release your anger.

---

12   1 Peter 2:23

Day 15:

Finding Serenity

Come to me, all who labor and are heavy laden, and I will give you rest. Take

my yoke upon you, and learn from me, for I am gentle and lowly in heart, and

you will find rest for your souls. For my yoke is easy, and my burden is light."

—Matthew 11:28-30

"PEACE BE WITH YOU"[2] WERE JESUS' FIRST words to His beloved disciples after rising from the dead. The very first words heard from the One who had seen the other side and come back again were words of peace. Pause for a moment and listen to the victorious Jesus as He still speaks those powerful words over you: "Peace be with you."

> [One's] believe the only way you'll know peace on the inside is if you perfect everything on the outside.
>
> –Cron and Stabile,
> *The Road Back To You*[1]

God knitted the world together in peace, connecting everyone and everything together with cords of love. Peace is just as foundational as the law of gravity, the

---

1   Cron and Stabile, *The Road Back to You*, 108.

2   John 20:19

hidden presence undergirding all creation and holding things together. It's not an idealistic hope for some time without strife but an active ingredient in the very fabric of creation. Like Eden, God created your life to be warm and loving, tranquil and perfectly calm.

We've spent plenty of time on the vices, the weaknesses of Improvers, but your greatest virtue is *serenity*. Serenity is an inward felt sense of goodness, wholeness, and completeness that doesn't hinge on circumstance. When in a state of serenity, relaxed in God's presence, you trust yourself, others, the process, and in God's sovereign control over all things. Serenity doesn't turn a blind eye to what needs improving, nor does it lower your standards, but it allows you to enjoy the world as it is *right now*. We are called to love this world, and true love, after all, is a commitment to the beloved in all states and times and conditions.

Serenity is something that must be *received*, not achieved. It's not forcing the river, but jumping in and going with the flow.[3] In fact, working harder to achieve more peace in your life is like a fish trying to get off a hook:

> Serenity is something that must be received, not achieved.

the more you struggle, the more deeply the hook gets driven in. Serenity is not found through seizing control, but rather in letting go of your attachments to the "right way" or "best practices." I heard a One share that for years she felt chained to her compulsions, which felt like a yoke around her neck. Her metaphor is striking considering Jesus' comforting words: "Come to me, all who labor and are heavy laden, and I will give you rest. Take my yoke upon you, and learn from me, for I am gentle and lowly in heart, and you will find rest for your souls. For my yoke is easy, and my burden is light."[4]

It's hard to imagine sometimes that Jesus' commands would be lighter than our compulsions; that His yoke fits more comfortably on our shoulders than our "shoulds." If we are humble enough to take Jesus' hand and walk with someone who is gentle and lowly rather than harsh and berating like your inner critic, the promise is that life will be easier and lighter. Doesn't that almost seem too good to be true? I know it's extremely hard to simply throw off the yoke of your

---

3 Wagner, *Nine Lenses on the World*, 164.

4 Matthew 11:28-30

compulsions, especially after it appears that being yoked to them has helped you pull the plow harder and faster, but you can do it. The repentance that leads to rest for Ones is not pulling more weight, but throwing off your yoke and taking Jesus' upon you."[5]

The Good News for Improvers is that you've been given a serenity that can withstand any circumstance. This is a peace that does more than simply calm the storm of chaos around you; it has the power to create a vibrant spirit of wholeness within you. Without the presence of God, serenity is impossible; with God, "The peace of God, which surpasses all understanding, will guard your hearts and your minds in Christ Jesus."[6] If you are tired and weary today, this promise stands: "I will give you rest."[7]

→ Pray

Father, help me let go of the yoke I've been carrying so that I can receive the peace You so desperately want to give me. Like Jesus asleep on the boat in the storm, help me know the kind of peace I can have on the inside when everything is imperfect on the outside. I'm ready to give up more control so that I can gain more rest. Reassure me that it'll be okay.

---

5 Matthew 11:29

6 Philippians 4:7

7 Matthew 11:28

Day 15 Reflections:

When have you experienced a serenity that made you think everything was as it should have been? Where were you? What were you doing?

_____

_____

_____

_____

To determine what compulsions have turned into obsessions, answer these fill-in-the-blanks: "I must ... " or "If I don't ... ."

_____

_____

_____

_____

What is yours to do right now? What is not yours to do?

_____

_____

_____

_____

→ Respond

Take a prayer walk in nature where you can let go of the voices of duty and simply receive from God in a place where you have no responsibility.

Day 16:

Progress over Perfection

You therefore must be perfect, as your heavenly Father is perfect.

—Matthew 5:48

IN THE BEGINNING, GOD SPOKE CREATION INTO existence and, upon observing the works of His hands, exclaimed, "it was very good."[2] Interestingly, "good" is a word Improvers don't have in their vocabulary, and when they hear it, they respond, "Yes, but we should be perfect as our heavenly Father is perfect!" As you can imagine, these words from Jesus have become somewhat of a life verse for perfectionists, however, stretching those words beyond their proper context has consequences.

> Perfectionism screams failure and hides progress.
>
> –Jon Acuff[1]

Pastor Ken Kovacs writes from his own experience: "I read in my Bible, 'Be perfect, therefore, as your heavenly Father is perfect.' There it is: I must be perfect—the Bible tells me so. To a child there's nothing ambiguous about the word 'perfect.' I knew it meant never making mistakes, being morally upright, pure, sinless,

---

1   Jonathan Acuff, *Finish: Give Yourself the Gift of Done* (New York, NY: Portfolio/Penguin, 2017), 124.

2   Genesis 1:31

beyond reproach. The hearing of this verse distorted a lot of things. It hindered my ability to hear anything about God's love. I had no understanding of grace. Looking back now, I see that my psyche co-opted this text and then used it to reinforce, justify, even 'sanctified' my skewed perspective of things."[3]

Yet, Jesus' words, "You therefore must be perfect,"[4] come with their own context—one we ignore to our own and others detriment. This verse can be misleading if we read it as a demand to live up to an impossible standard. But if we translate the Greek word *telios* (τέλειος)[5] (usually rendered as "perfect") in this verse as *mature, full grown,* or *fully completed,* Jesus' command becomes more clear: to exercise a more mature or full grown love than the Gentiles show one another. The *telios* (perfect) love of Christ—which He showed to its *telios,* its fullest extent[6]—is the sort that "drives out fear," that "always trusts, always hopes, always perseveres."[7]

When the rich young man came to Jesus asking, "What do I still lack?" Jesus replied, "If you would be perfect [*teleios*], go, sell what you possess and give to the poor. "[8] Once again, Jesus wasn't

> Good is progress, not perfection.

demanding perfection in the sense of being without fault, but rather showing him where his spiritual maturity was lacking.[9] Don't buy into the crazy idea that perfection can be achieved in this life and let yourself feel like a constant failure when you fall short. Instead, let God redefine your definition of good. Good is *progress,* not perfection. It is seeking your own life's *telios,* and guiding others toward theirs.

Doesn't this change pretty much change everything? You can put away the attitude that says, "If you can't do it perfectly the first time, don't bother doing

---

3   Ken Kovacs, "Wholeness, Not Perfection," On the Way, March 24, 2019, https://kekovacs.blogspot.com/2019/03/wholeness-not-perfection.html.

4   Matthew 5:48

5   Strong's Greek: 5046. τέλειος (TELEIOS), accessed April 20, 2022, https://biblehub.com/greek/5046.htm.

6   John 13:1

7   1 John 4:18 NIV; 1 Corinthians 13:7 NIV

8   Matthew 19:20-21

9   Similarly, the apostle Paul uses different variations of *telios* in his letters which get translated as "maturity." See 1 Corinthians 14:20, Colossians 1:28, Ephesians 4:13, and Philippians 3:15 for examples.

it at all" and start to adopt the mentality that "done is better than perfect," and "perfect is the enemy of the good." You no longer have to treat every decision or conversation like a grand recital performance, preparing for every eventuality in your mind until you get it down perfectly. You can show people your unedited thoughts and rough drafts—you can be *human*.

The Good News for Improvers is that you can patiently enjoy progress because Jesus has already fulfilled your longing for perfection. The author of Hebrews says of Jesus, "For by a single offering he has perfected for all time those who are being sanctified."[10] In other words, when it comes to our salvation, we have been declared perfect in God's eyes although we are still being perfected by Him. Through Christ, God has always-already done—brought to completion—what was necessary to bring us near. Though we are unpolished jars of clay, we can still point others to the divine treasure within "to show that the surpassing power belongs to God and not to us."[11] Because you are loved *and* still a work in progress, go and show others that same grace today and let what is "good enough" be good enough.

→ Pray

Father, thank You for giving me a thirst for perfection, for things to be as they ought to be. Now, give me Your patience. Just as you delight in a young child learning to play the violin with all the scratching and squeaking, so do You delight in my every effort. Help me to see not only what *ought* to be, but what *can* be—and to celebrate every small step along the way to completion.

---

10   Hebrews 10:14

11   2 Corinthians 4:7

Day 16 Reflections:

Who or what reinforced the idea that you need to be perfect?

_____

_____

_____

_____

What is beautiful about your flaws? How has God used them?

_____

_____

_____

_____

How can you celebrate progress and small wins more?

_____

_____

_____

_____

→ Respond

Practice showing others your "rough drafts." Whether it's a literal rough draft of a creative project or an undeveloped thought or idea, know that it doesn't have to be perfect right away to be good.[12]

---

12   Sarajane Case, _The Honest Enneagram: Know Your Type, Own Your Challenges, Embrace Your Growth_ (Kansas City, MO: Andrews McMeel Publishing, 2020), 48.

Day 17:

Aiming for the Bullseye

Not that I have already obtained this or am already perfect, but I press on to

make it my own, because Christ Jesus has made me his own.

—Philippians 3:12

WHEN YOU SEE SOMETHING THAT MATCHES YOUR ideal of perfection are you overcome with joy? Perhaps it's a sunset, piece of music, or a plan perfectly executed. Much like the great ancient philosopher, Plato, you hold a beautiful vision of the way the world should be—of the ideal behind the faulty reality. As your friends, family, and teammates, we realize how difficult it must be for you to get so close to your visions of the ideal only to have it so consistently melt away.

> **Perfection is like an ice sculpture: it lasts only as long as there's no change in the atmosphere.**
>
> –Suzanne Stabile[1]

Have you struggled in the past when you didn't get that perfect grade or execute that project flawlessly? I know it can be hard for you not to feel like a failure when you miss the bullseye. As discussed yesterday, the way we read the Bible can reinforce the belief that we are

---

1   Suzanne Stabile, *The Path Between Us: An Enneagram Journey to Healthy Relationships* (Downers Grove, IL: InterVarsity Press, 2018), 61.

failures. For example, if you've been around the church, you've probably heard that the English word *sin* is an archery term, and that anything we do outside the bullseye is to fall far short of God's intended purpose. While this is true to an extent, this illustration is meant to show us our need for a Savior, not to paralyze us with a failure mentality.

Keeping that in mind, I want to assure you that it's okay to *aim* for the bullseye. Though the apostle Paul knew he would never be perfect in this life, it didn't stop him from trying: "Not that I have already obtained this or am already perfect, but I press on to make it my own, because Christ Jesus has made me his own."[2] Therein lies an encouragement for all Ones: Paul, not taking God's grace for granted, worked *harder* than anyone.[3] He saw the beauty of simplicity, of not allowing the ideal to stop him from enjoying the good. But it didn't stop him from pursuing the ideal, either.

When you aim for the bullseye, it pushes all of us to do better—just don't expect us to hit the bullseye every time. Cast a perfect vision, but don't expect perfect results. There's a big difference between perfectionism and high-performance. A culture of perfectionism makes unreasonable demands for time and energy, creates unnecessary bottlenecks, delays projects, and produces a loss of self-esteem. You will burn others (or yourself) out if you spend the whole weekend trying to get a project from "excellent" to "perfect." On the other hand, a culture of high-performance also champions high standards, attention to detail, and a commitment to quality and excellence. In the end, the difference is *grace*. As the civil rights leader and lawyer Mahatma Gandhi said, "Freedom is not worth having if it does not include the freedom to make mistakes."[4]

> Cast a perfect vision, but don't expect perfect results.

The growth path for Ones includes turning unattainable standards into realistic goals; turning "I want to be good" or "We can do better" into achievable steps so that you can celebrate when you've attained them. Additionally, try lowering

---

2   Philippians 3:12

3   1 Corinthians 15:10

4   Beatrice Chestnut, *The Complete Enneagram: 27 Paths to Greater Self-Knowledge* (Berkeley, CA: She Writes Press, 2013).

the bar in some areas of life to improve other ones. I once had a friend tell me he wished he would've gotten more B's in college because he spent all of his free time studying. Although receiving A's came with much satisfaction, he later regretted not spending more time making new friends and growing the ones he did have.

The Good News for Improvers is that you don't have to create (or keep) higher standards than everyone else to feel a sense of worth. You will naturally find your standards higher than most, but your standards are just that: *yours*. Neither God nor your fellow humans expect perfection. My heart is aching for you to see that no matter how many times you miss the mark, you are always and forever in the center of God's unconditional love and acceptance. In the game of life, every outer-circle surrounding the bullseye has value. God sees the targets you are hitting and wants you to know they all count for something! Therefore, relax and let *joy*, not the bullseye, be your main motivator in all you do.

→ Pray

Father, I appreciate all the moments of pure bliss You've given me. Thank You for using me to raise the bar for myself and those around me to achieve great things. Help me to meditate today on the fact that Jesus' motivation for enduring the cross was "joy."[5] Let joy be my inward motivator and outward expression as I run my race here on earth.

---

5   Hebrews 12:2

Day 17 Reflections:

When have your high standards benefited you or others?

_____

_____

_____

_____

Is joy or obligation your primary motivator?

_____

_____

_____

_____

What can you do to create a grace-driven, but still high-performance culture?

_____

_____

_____

_____

➜ Respond

Big standards start with small steps. Start a ten-minute daily workout, set a goal to pay off a specific amount of debt, make a call to a counselor, or help your team write down some critical path steps toward a goal.

Day 18:

Stress Triggers

And Moses lifted up his hand and struck the rock with his staff twice, and water

came out abundantly, and the congregation drank, and their livestock. And the

LORD said to Moses and Aaron, "Because you did not believe in me, to uphold

me as holy in the eyes of the people of Israel, therefore you shall not bring this

assembly into the land that I have given them."

—Numbers 20:11-12

WE ALL GET STRESSED FROM TIME TO time, but if we don't pay attention to the warning signs, we will find ourselves at the breaking point quickly—or maybe even in a public meltdown. Beth McCord shares some of the most common triggers that may lead to a blow up for the Improver, such as being criticized or scrutinized; seeing people being deceptive, irresponsible, and lazy; or knowing people are not taking responsibility or are failing to complete their responsibilities with precision and accuracy.[2] Other stressors may include

No pressure, no diamonds.

–Thomas Carlyle[1]

---

1   Iam A. Freeman, *Seeds of Revolution: A Collection of Axioms, Passages and Proverbs, Volume 1* (Bloomington, IN: iUniverse,World Harvest, 2014), 74.

2   McCord and McCord, *Becoming Us.*

observing people break the rules, ignore manners, act unethically, make excuses, dismiss important details, or arrive late to meetings.

When you experience these stressors, you may immediately feel judgment, self-righteous anger, and a desire to withdraw into a melancholy state. Ones appear outwardly calm most of the time, but the anger and stress are slowly building within. But given enough time, even the strongest pressure cookers will finally explode. Some of the warning signs that you are turning into a walking steam kettle are that you become inflexible on your positions, act self-righteously, rationalize and justify bad behavior, feel disillusioned and depressed, turn obsessive and compulsive, or masochistically punish yourself.[3] Unhealthy Ones will consistently display outbursts of rage such as throwing dishes, slamming doors, or exploding in critical tirades.[4]

The Bible presents many case studies of people who shut down completely or lashed out in a public meltdown because of stress. One of those whose failures were very visible (and came with steep consequences) is Moses. More than once, he seems to throw up his hands, telling God he would rather die than deal with the unfaithful Israelites another moment. While the shutdowns often occur in private, Moses's public meltdowns took place before the entire nation—like the one at Meribah, when he struck the rock.[5]

> Because God has a long fuse, He doesn't react, retaliate, or punish quickly, but is merciful and forbearing.

Moses had a very stressful job—in the hot desert for over forty years, no less!—so it's understandable that he sometimes bent past the breaking point. He had to deal with the constant complaining, bickering, and backsliding of an entire nation and is somehow supposed to always know what to do. Not only that, but his leadership and authority were under constant threat by his own friends and family. We hear often of Moses's self-doubt, frustration, loneliness, and anger, and his final public failure at Meribah is the stated reason he was denied entry

---

3   Riso and Hudson, *The Wisdom of the Enneagram*, 116-117.

4   Maitri, *The Spiritual Dimension of the Enneagram*, 121.

5   Numbers 20:10-13

to the promised land. Nonetheless, Moses always recovered and stood with his people, faithfully leading them to the doorstep of Canaan, and he is known as the greatest prophet in Jewish history.

The Good News for Improvers is that there is a way to bend without breaking. You are loved by a God who is "merciful and gracious, slow to anger and abounding in steadfast love and faithfulness."[6] He is long-suffering toward us, meaning He is willing to wait with patience long before showing anger. Because He has a long fuse, God doesn't react, retaliate, or punish quickly, but is merciful and forbearing. He is also willing to give you a longer fuse so you can act honorably before all and "uphold [God] as holy in the eyes of the people"[7]—the very thing Moses failed to do at Meribah. Let your stress lead to sanctification—a cleansing. Just as Jesus received the world's hostility on the cross and yet reverberated love in a remarkable demonstration of self-control, you too can pour out grace on even the most irresponsible and lazy people you know.

The next time you feel the kettle getting hot, assume the best about people first and foremost. Remember, not everyone is wired like you. Seek to ask clarifying questions instead of making judgmental statements. If someone was in the wrong, seek to forgive quickly and release any resentment. Finally and most importantly, trust that the Holy Spirit will keep doing His work in them.[8] Remember, they may make mistakes, but God still loves them!

→ Pray

Father, thank You for sending Your Son to be our example of someone who bent without breaking. Through temptation, opposition, persecution, and even death, He did not fold. Oh Lord, let the same compassion flow out of me that flowed out of Jesus when He was struck on the cross.

---

6   Psalm 86:15

7   Numbers 20:12

8   McCord and McCord, *Becoming Us.*

Day 18 Reflections:

What triggers your stress most often? What past stressful experiences might actually be diagnosed as trauma?

_____

_____

_____

_____

Describe a time when you could have lashed out at someone who deserved it but instead were slow to anger, merciful, and gracious.

_____

_____

_____

_____

What steps can you take now to prevent a public meltdown like the one Moses experienced?

_____

_____

_____

_____

→ Respond

Because others may be able to see the warning signs before you do, ask someone to share how they can tell when you are stressed out.

Day 19:

Seeking Reform

The law of the Lord is perfect, reviving the soul; the testimony of the Lord

is sure, making wise the simple; the precepts of the Lord are right, rejoicing

the heart; the commandment of the Lord is pure, enlightening the eyes; the

fear of the Lord is clean, enduring forever; the rules of the Lord are true,

and righteous altogether.

—Psalm 19:7-9

If you want a job as an Outdoor Guide, I hear you must have good people skills, a passion for teaching others, enjoy being in nature, and love doing the actual work of hiking, biking, backpacking, or rafting alongside the people you are leading. This seems like the perfect job for an Improver: in a way, you are already our guide in life, serving as a moral compass pointing us in the right direction. I love that you seek to put principles over preferences.

> Always stand on principle even if you stand alone.
>
> –John Adams

Riso and Hudson explain, "In civic life, for example, [Improvers] vote their consciences rather than their pocketbooks. As parents, they decide issues on the basis of what will benefit the entire community rather than what will favor only their own children. As religious persons, they act on their religious principles, even if it means disobeying civil authorities. However, Ones can be extremely courageous in this regard, jeopardizing themselves, their possessions, their reputations, even their lives for their principles."[1]

The definition of a moral compass includes more than simply determining what is right and wrong, but also the ability to discern how to act accordingly.[2] Ones demonstrate this in the way they pursue both private change and public action.[3] One such leader in Scripture was King Josiah. Following the death of Solomon, the Kingdom of Israel was divided in two and most of the followers of Yahweh began worshiping false gods and descending into gross iniquity. Years later, Josiah became king of a nation falling short of its purpose to be a light for the world, and then he began a project of spiritual and physical reconstruction. During this time, "the Book of the Law" was found in the Temple after being lost in their minds and hearts for many years.[4] After hearing it read out loud for the first time, Josiah's response was visceral: he tore his clothes as a sign of repentance and mourned over how far his people had departed from God's way.

> Ones pursue private change and public action.

Taking immediate action and stewarding his God-given privilege and power as king, Josiah initiated sweeping reforms that affected every sphere of culture and lasted over a decade.[5] During a time of grave moral decay following a long line of indifferent and irresponsible leaders, Josiah was a breath of fresh air. It was said, "Before him there was no king like him, who turned to the Lord with all his heart and with all his soul and with all his might, according to all the Law of Moses, nor did any like him arise after him."[6]

---

1 Riso and Hudson, *Personality Types*, 389.

2 "Moral Compass," Oxford Lexico, accessed April 20, 2022, https://www.lexico.com/en/definition/moral_compass.

3 See the appendix *Three Types of Improvers*.

4 2 Kings 22:8,11,13

5 2 Kings 22:12–23:32

6 2 Kings 23:25

Like Josiah, the Bible is a powerful tool in the hand of a One who wants things on earth to be as it is in heaven. It has guided God's people across the millennia, offering insight and a language for how we ought to teach, correct, and train others.[7] The Word of God is perfect, pure, dependable, soul-reviving, wisdom-imparting, mind-enlightening, heart-rejoicing, and life-altering.[8]

The Good News for Improvers is that through Christ we have access to a revelation deeper even than the written word of Scripture: the living Word of God—the incarnate Divine, who "became flesh and blood, and moved into the neighborhood."[9] Just as Josiah removed the idols from the land, you too can use the Bible to inspire people to let go of personal idols such as sex, money, power, health, and image or cultural idols such as nationalism, consumerism, racism, sexism, individualism, intellectualism, or any other -ism you can think of. It won't be easy, but it'll be worth it. Remember Jesus, the ultimate Improver, who didn't just live courageously for His principles, but died keeping them. Now, from His throne in heaven and in each of our hearts, He declares, "Behold, I am making all things new."[10]

→ Pray

Father, Your Word is an illuminating lamp, lighting our way in times of moral darkness. Like Jesus, help me never to sacrifice my principles and make compromises. Thank You for giving me a zeal to take action when I see the world through Your eyes. Now, give me Josiah's courage to do something about it.

---

7   2 Timothy 3:16

8   Psalm 19:7-9

9   John 1:14 MSG

10   Revelation 21:5

Day 19 Reflections:

Why do you appreciate the Bible? How has it helped you to accomplish what God's called you to do?

_____

_____

_____

_____

When was the last time you felt like "tearing your clothes" over the spiritual state of your soul or this nation?

_____

_____

_____

_____

What personal or cultural idols listed above grieve your heart? What changes would you like to enforce if you had the time and resources?

_____

_____

_____

_____

➔ Respond

Seek to join a group of people, church, non-profit, or organization to team up with that aligns with your desires for moral or ethical reform.

Day 20:

False Righteousness

For his sake I have suffered the loss of all things and count them as rubbish, in order that I may gain Christ and be found in him, not having a righteousness of my own that comes from the law, but that which comes through faith in Christ, the righteousness from God that depends on faith ...

—Philippians 3:8b-9

AT THE TENDER AGE OF THIRTEEN, MARTIN Luther's parents sent him to sixteenth century boarding school to become a lawyer. However, after almost dying in a lightning storm, Luther had a deeply spiritual experience and changed careers, entering the priesthood instead—and changed the world forever.

> Grace is not opposed to effort, it is opposed to earning.
>
> –Dallas Willard[1]

Throughout Luther's childhood he never felt good enough, unable to fully measure up before a righteous God, and even as an adult priest and seminary professor, his soul was tormented daily, feeling *unqualified* for ministry. But during a season while he was

---

1   Dallas Willard, *The Great Omission: Reclaiming Jesus's Essential Teachings on Discipleship* (San Francisco, CA: HarperSanFrancisco, 2006), 61.

studying and lecturing on the book of Romans, he had a dramatic conversion experience. He recalled, "At last, by the mercy of God, meditating day and night … I began to understand that the righteousness of God is that by which the righteous lives by a gift of God, namely by faith. … Here I felt that I was altogether born again and had entered paradise itself through open gates."[2] With a newfound sense of freedom, Martin Luther became fully convinced that God's saving grace was not something we could merit, and sought to reform the Roman Catholic church's teachings, but was eventually excommunicated and continued his work in the burgeoning Protestant Reformation.[3]

The Reformation, led by Luther and others, put the doctrine of justification (i.e., how we are made right with God) on center stage. It was taught that Christ's righteousness is *imputed* (credited to our spiritual account all at once), rather than being *infused* (small payments over time), and that God declared us righteous *instantly* when we received Christ as Savior, not *progressively* as we become more good. Thus, Luther's most famous Latin phrase became *simul justus et peccator,* meaning to be simultaneously justified/righteous *and* a sinner.[4]

> When we drift from the good news, we go back to a merit-based system of earning our righteousness.

When we drift from this good news, we go back to a merit-based system of earning our righteousness—a default that, while familiar to us all, is unfortunately all too common with Ones. We all have our go-to false sources of righteousness that we use to prove ourselves. Check out these helpful examples from *The Gospel-Centered Life* study[5]:

• Job righteousness: "God will reward me because I work the hardest."

---

2   Martin Luther and John Dillenberger, *Martin Luther Selections from His Writings* (Garden City, NY: Anchor Books, Doubleday, 1961), 11.

3   History.com Editors, "Martin Luther and the 95 Theses," History.com (A&E Television Networks, October 29, 2009), https://www.history.com/topics/reformation/martin-luther-and-the-95-theses.

4   "What Does 'Simul Justus et Peccator' Mean?," Ligonier Ministries, October 17, 2019, https://www.ligonier.org/posts/simul-justus-et-peccator.

5   Robert H. Thune and Will Walker, *The Gospel-Centered Life: Study Guide with Leader's Notes* (Greensboro, NC: New Growth Press, 2016).

- Theological righteousness: "God prefers me over those who have bad theology."

- Intellectual righteousness: "I am superior because I am smarter and more articulate."

- Schedule righteousness: "I am more mature because of my rigorous self-discipline and time management."

- Legalistic righteousness: "I am better because I don't drink, smoke, chew, or date guys/gals who do."

- Financial righteousness: "Unlike most people, I manage my money wisely and stay out of debt."

The list goes on. A false source of righteousness can be any talent, effort, or achievement we depend on to make ourselves feel more *self*-righteous. It might not even be driven by a conscious desire for superiority, but rather be an unconscious desire to cover up our insecurities. Whatever our motives, when we wander from the gospel of grace to live in a spiritual meritocracy instead, the result is either shame (when we are failing) or pride (when we are succeeding). Living in this volatile system, where your divine worth is always increasing and decreasing as quickly as the stock market, leads to what Luther described as a tortured soul.

The Good News for Improvers is that you don't need to submit a spiritual resume or performance evaluation for God to accept (and keep accepting) you. In fact, the apostle Paul ripped up his resume, filled with all kinds of worldly sources of righteousness, so that he could gain Christ. After the road to Damascus, the Father no longer looked at him through the lens of his merits or demerits, but rather through the lens of His perfect Son! The beautiful thing about being a Christ-follower is, as Chrystal Evans Hurst says, "You are allowed to be both a masterpiece and a work in progress simultaneously."[6] Therefore, remember that what is needed today to combat a negative self-esteem isn't a more righteous view of yourself but an accurate view of yourself hidden in the love of Christ. That is liberating.

---

6   Chrystal Evans Hurst, *She's Still There: Rescuing the Girl in You* (Grand Rapids, MI: Zondervan, 2017).

→ Pray

Father, You know I want to be good but sometimes I take it too far. Help me to catch myself in the act when I'm dwelling on what I'm doing better than others. Because Christ leveled the playing field on the cross, I will neither lavish nor withhold love and acceptance from others on a success/fail basis. Today, I will choose to see others as saints, not sinners.

Day 20 Reflections:

Who has shown you unconditional love whether you were at your best or your worst?

_____

_____

_____

With help from the list above, what false sources of righteousness have you relied on the most and why?

_____

_____

_____

What are some practical ways you can treat sinners like masterpieces?

_____

_____

_____

→ Respond

Write out a short three- to five-minute testimony to share with others, articulating how Jesus saved you from self-righteousness.

Day 21:

Grace Party

... but he answered his father, "Look, these many years I have served you, and I never disobeyed your command, yet you never gave me a young goat, that I might celebrate with my friends. But when this son of yours came, who has devoured your property with prostitutes, you killed the fattened calf for him!"

—Luke 15:29-30

IMPROVERS CAN MAKE INCREDIBLE PARENTS, CAREGIVERS, AND mentors. Author Jacqui Pollock explains healthy Ones are conscientious leaders, instilling values in their home like honesty, integrity, and responsibility. You set clear boundaries for everyone, making life much more predictable. You create order and structure, alleviating others' stress. You are detail-oriented, planning fun activities and outings (the one who always packs more than we need!). When conflict arises, you help everyone break down the issues, come to a clear

> One of the hardest things in the world is to stop being the prodigal son without turning into the elder brother.
>
> –John Ortberg[1]

---

1   John Ortberg, *The Life You've Always Wanted: Spiritual Disciplines for Ordinary People* (Grand Rapids, MI: Zondervan, 2009), 113.

understanding of the problem, and discern the best possible solutions. Focused on your own self-improvement, you are a paragon of virtue: a role model raising the bar for your family, friends, and mentees.[2]

But there is always a shadow. Pollock goes on to explain the negative effects of an unhealthy One: being overly attached to perfection, you can create unrealistic expectations—for yourself and others. While such unattainable goals lead you to keep striving, it can be demoralizing for others and lead to burnout and relational breakdown. A stressed One may get overly tense and anxious in their bodies, take things too seriously, become demanding, or get stuck in the details, stifling the free thinking and creativity of those around them. Unhealthy Ones also tend to become overly opinionated, upset when they don't feel properly appreciated, or defensive when others try to confront them; others have excuses, but Ones have *reasons why* their opinions and actions are actually correct.[3]

Let's now look at some strategies for growing as a parent, caregiver, or mentor: Be more flexible, remembering that there is typically more than one right way to do anything. Practice good listening, remembering to ask for (and act on!) the opinions of others and

> Don't stay outside judging the prodigals in your life, but come into the party of grace.

encourage open-ended discussions on different viewpoints. Be more patient, talking openly and calmly about what is making you angry rather than blaming or accusing. Use more humor so that those around you can experience your fun, lighter side. Lastly, be more *imperfect*, admitting and confessing your failures to create a grace-filled home where it's ok to make mistakes![4]

One of the best stories for Ones to meditate on is the parable of the Prodigal Son.[5] It's about a grace-filled father raising two very different sons in his home. The younger, having a "grass is greener" mentality, went off to a distant land to

---

2   Tracy Tresidder, Margaret Loftus, and Jacqui Pollock, Knowing Me, Knowing Them: Understand Your Parenting Personality by Discovering the Enneagram (Carlton North, Vic.: Monterey Press, 2014), 50-51.

3   Ibid, 51-52.

4   Ibid, 56-58.

5   Luke 15:11-32

find happiness. Once there, he squandered away all of his father's inheritance as quick as a bad trip to Vegas. Dirt poor, sitting among the pigs, he had a spiritual awakening and journeyed back home in shame to his father. Unexpectedly, the father had been waiting for his return and ran toward him, kissed and hugged him, covered up his rags with the best robe in the house, put shoes on his blistered feet, and slid the family ring on his hand.

Meanwhile, the older brother, in typical unhealthy One fashion, threw a pious tantrum. When the father hosted a welcome home feast, the older brother refused to go in and join the party. He couldn't believe his irresponsible brother, who broke every rule in the family playbook, was getting off the hook. The father's grace, in his mind, was undeserved, unfair, and nowhere close to *good*.

This parable, told by Jesus to the morally superior Pharisees, was intended to show them that their obedience was really for *them*, not out of love for the Father. Here we are reminded that Jesus' strongest critiques were not reserved for the younger brother types—those who appeared to be "living in sin"—but for the elder brothers: for the people of faith who thought their right actions were what made them lovable to the father.

The Good News for Improvers is that the Father doesn't hold grudges, but extends grace to both prodigals *and* self-righteous older brothers. As you go about your day today, picture your heavenly Father with a smile on His face, waving His arms, inviting you to come in and watch how He loves all His children, both the good and the bad ones. If you've been pursued and wrapped up in the arms of your gracious Father, don't stay outside judging the prodigals in your life—come into the party of grace.

→ Pray

Father, thank You for giving me a one-track mind when it comes to helping family and friends. I love the way I'm wired. Now, help me show others the same kind of undeserved grace You've shown me. When I feel a grudge coming on, give me the Spirit's power to release my anger and forgive quickly. Use me to establish a home where grace reigns above all.

Day 21 Reflections:

When was the last time the Father ran toward you and covered you with grace?

_____

_____

_____

_____

What do you need to sacrifice or let go of to throw a grace party for someone who doesn't deserve it?

_____

_____

_____

_____

Which strength above has made a positive impact on your family, friends, or someone else? Which growth strategy above would you like to focus on next and why?

_____

_____

_____

_____

➙ Respond

Pursue a prodigal in your life and hit the refresh button by sending them an encouraging note or an invitation to dinner.

Day 22:

Reaction Formation

My frame was not hidden from you, when I was being made in secret,

intricately woven in the depths of the earth.

—Psalm 139:15

FRED MCFEELY ROGERS WAS THE HOST OF the popular preschool television series *Mister Rogers' Neighborhood*, which ran on public television for thirty-three years. This host, producer, and Presbyterian minister had a remarkable way of helping children identify and work through their emotions using song and puppets. The man was a machine of dependability: Every morning at 5:30 a.m., Fred woke up, went for a swim, read his Bible, and responded to the thousands of letters he received from children, praying for each child by name.

> The greatest gift you ever give is your honest self.
> —Fred Rogers[1]

He would then arrive at the studio for work, only stopping for an afternoon nap. After arriving home, he would go to bed exactly at 9:30 p.m.[2] He also never deviated from weighing exactly 143

---

1 Fred Rogers, *You Are Special: Words of Wisdom for All Ages from a Beloved Neighbor* (New York, NY: Penguin Publishing Group, 1995), 118.

2 Rachel Chang, "Mister Rogers Consistently Weighed 143 Pounds. the Significance behind That Number," Biography. com (A&E Networks Television, December 15, 2020), https://www.biography.com/news/mister-rogers-143-i-love-you.

pounds because of its symbolic reminder to spread love: "I" (one letter), "love" (four letters), and "you" (three letters). 1-4-3.

Fred, like a healthy One, turned his anger into action, exercising regularly and channeling his keen sense of justice through his work. But few people ever saw him get angry. Noah Harpster, a screenwriter for the movie *A Beautiful Day In The Neighborhood* starring Tom Hanks said, "The two most important people in Fred's life both say that he didn't talk to them, he didn't share the burden that he was taking on all day. Where did that go?"[3]

In Enneagram theory, Improvers are said to have a defense mechanism called *reaction formation,* which makes someone do the opposite of how they feel to shield themselves from internal or external criticism. A One may act extremely nice to

> Keep banging on those low keys, and wait till we're by your side.

someone they want to confront. If a One feels racist or thinks they are perceived to be so, they may take a public stand or join a cause to prove they aren't. When Ones feel any "unacceptable" emotion in their body, their mind intercepts this impulse, judges it, and says, "No Way Jose!"[4] Therefore, Ones unconsciously push their unacceptable emotions down like a beach ball underwater, presenting themselves in a more socially "acceptable" way.

While being the "good" person doesn't sound like a bad thing, there's a high cost to ignoring the negative end of your emotions. For starters, it keeps you from doing your inner-work, paying attention to the flares you send out to redirect missiles of criticism. In addition, when you are too proper, it prevents intimacy between you and those who want to see the *whole* you. This is where you can take a few cues from a healthy Four, the personality type that expresses their full range of emotions, and get in touch with the deep desire to be fully known by others just as God knows us.

---

3   Jason Tabrys, "The Final Lesson from 'A Beautiful Day in the Neighborhood' Is One Worth Holding Onto," (UPROXX, February 7, 2020), https://uproxx.com/movies/a-beautiful-day-in-the-neighborhood-lesson/.

4   Chestnut, *The Complete Enneagram.*

The Good News for Improvers is that God loves your whole self, not the superpolite version you present to others. From the womb, God sees every part of you behind the "good boy" and "good girl" mask. As the Psalmist says, "My frame was not hidden from you, when I was being made in secret, intricately woven in the depths of the earth."[5] Keeping the mask on indefinitely will only perpetuate the lie that you are not loved for who you really are, but how good you appear to be. You are the one Christ lived and died for, and with Him you never have to be someone else.

Fred Rogers said that one healthy way to deal with negative feelings is to bang on the low keys of a piano. That is why the final scene of *A Beautiful Day In The Neighborhood* is such a memorable one: Fred sits alone at the piano, the show is over and the studio is empty. He begins to play, then pounds a few times on the low keys in frustration. He pauses for a few seconds, regains his composure, and resumes his peaceful song.

While there is much to admire about Fred's work, the final scene left me wanting more of "low key" Fred. The world is longing to see the minor keys that make up the melody behind your amazing work. Those closest to you want—*need*—to hear the low notes that are the driving force behind all the good you're doing. Keep banging on those low keys and trust us to sing along.

→ Pray

Father, thank You for loving the person behind the mask I've presented to others. As someone who strives to be honest with the truth, help me also to be authentic with my emotions. Give me the courage to show the world a different tune—one that allows others to hear both the high notes and the low notes of my life.

---

5   Psalm 139:15

Day 22 Reflections:

What's inspiring to you about Fred Rogers' life and legacy?

_____

_____

_____

_____

Where do you see evidence of "reaction formation" in your life? What activates it?

_____

_____

_____

How will you expand your definition of goodness to include heartfelt authenticity? What's stopping you?

_____

_____

_____

_____

➜ Respond

Tell someone today what's bothering you, even if it makes you uncomfortable.

Day 23:

Connection over Perfection

And Jesus said to them, "I ask you, is it lawful on the Sabbath to do good or to

do harm, to save life or to destroy it?" And after looking around at them all he

said to him, "Stretch out your hand." And he did so, and his hand was restored.

—Luke 6:9-10

DO YOU EVER GET SO FOCUSED ON your tasks that you forget *people* are the point? Make no mistake: the world needs "taskers." Families, companies, and churches need women and men who have checklists, plans, goals, and solutions; people who can stay focused and get things done quickly and with quality. For Improvers, the world is a disorganized, undeveloped mess just waiting for someone to swoop in and create order. They streamline organizations, create high-functioning teams, and increase productivity.

> The legacy of your life will not be judged by how many emails you responded to. . . . It will be measured, I believe, by how interruptible you were.
>
> –Jeff Goins[1]

---

1   Jeff Goins, "Please, Interrupt Me [Slow down Challenge: Day 4]," Jeff Goins, August 15, 2013, https://goinswriter.com/interrupt-me/.

The problem, however, arises when perfection is prioritized over people.

Enneagram teacher Suzanne Stabile teaches that Ones' relationships suffer when they habitually try to knock stuff off their to-do list and can't relax around others. In her book *The Path Between Us*, Stabile tells the story of Mary, who confessed to her, "So, if I'm in the house, whether I'm saying anything or not, and I'm all jittery because I know I still have a couple of things on my to-do list, I can't be still. There is no reason why those things couldn't be done tomorrow. They don't have to be done today, but I'm thinking, 'I have a little block of time and I should get that thing done.' When I respond to that urge to keep doing, I send a message to everyone in my household that they can't relax either. 'If I'm working you guys need to be working. If I'm not calm you guys can't be calm either.' "[2]

Stabile explains this task-tailspin: "Because Ones came to believe that meeting the expectations of others would, in some way, make them more valuable and offer them some much-desired security, relationships

> The pursuit of perfection can get in the way of connection.

became more about performing well than relating well and loving well."[3]

In the Bible, the Pharisees display a performance mindset, prioritizing the *law* over love. In Luke 6, the Pharisees harped on Jesus and His disciples for eating some heads of grain on the Sabbath because they were hungry. Jesus pointed them back to the time David bent the rules, doing a similar thing for his hungry followers.[4] On another Sabbath, the Pharisees watched like hawks, waiting to see if Jesus would heal a man with a withered hand. Perceiving their thoughts, He said, "I ask you, is it lawful on the Sabbath to do good or to do harm, to save life or to destroy it?"[5] Jesus rightfully rebuked them, pointing out that their zealousness for the law was getting in the way of simply loving people.

We are called as humans to be God's stewards of creation—and that includes people. We are not striving for perfection, but rather to perfect our love for all

2 Stabile, *The Path Between Us*, 67-68.

3 Ibid, 68-69.

4 Luke 6:1-5

5 Luke 6:9

that God has made. The pursuit of perfection can get in the way of connection, so as you diligently put in your best effort every day, make sure to save enough energy for those you care about. If you overdo it trying to perfect yourself or the world, you won't have anything left for the emotional needs of others.[6]

The Good News for Improvers is Jesus doesn't get so caught up in His work that he forgets to stop and care for us. For Him, *people* are the task: "the Sabbath is made for man, not man for the Sabbath."[7] Over and over again, Jesus focused on the *who* rather than the *what,* giving us a perfect example for how we ourselves ought to go about our work. All we have to do is stop and remember that God prioritizes us every day, not because we are useful, but because we are valuable. And He asks us to look at our relationships in the same way, as "spiritual unions" rather than business partners.[8] Too often, those in relationship with a One can feel like they are merely a box for the One to check. Therefore, as you work on that clean house, big project, lesson plan, ledger, or presentation, remember that, while those are all great things, they aren't the point: people are.

→ Pray

Father, You created me so that I might know You, but I lose my way when I believe I'm only useful to You when I'm improving things. Forgive me for being so overly focused on what I need to do that I forget who is with me. Help me take my eyes off myself and my checklist to be present with You and others. Enable me by Your Holy Spirit to be productively loving.

---

6   Stabile, *The Path Between Us*, 67.

7   Mark 2:27

8   Cron and Stabile, *The Road Back to You*, 140.

Day 23 Reflections:

How do you treat people when your get-it-done mode kicks into full gear?

_____

_____

_____

_____

Who or what is getting sacrificed right now for your tasks (marriage, kids, staff team, health, etc.)?

_____

_____

_____

_____

How will your day look different knowing God values connection over perfection?

_____

_____

_____

_____

→ Respond

Plan twenty-five percent less work this week than you normally do to allow for more spontaneous connections. If you budget more relational time, you'll be less stressed when "divine interruptions" come your way.

Day 24:

Living with Integrity

Whoever walks in integrity walks securely, but he who makes his ways crooked

will be found out.

—Proverbs 10:9

ON JUNE 24, 2021, A TWELVE-STORY BEACHFRONT condominium in Miami called Champlain Towers South collapsed, leaving ninety-eight people dead. As the third-deadliest structural engineering failure in United States history, an investigation was launched and found that the original design violated building codes at the time of construction in the 1970s. Compounded with decades of inattentiveness, the investigators realized that it was only a matter of time before collapse. How many casualties could've been prevented if shortcuts hadn't been taken on day one?[1]

> **Whenever you do a thing, act as if all the world were watching.**
>
> –Thomas à Kempis

Enneagram Threes like me are tempted to cut corners in life when efficiency and speed are of ultimate concern. An unhealthy Three will do something

---

1   Sarah Blaskey, Aaron Leibowitz, and Ben Conarck, "Design of Collapsed Condo Was Weak and ... - Miamiherald. com," Miami Herald, January 21, 2022, https://www.miamiherald.com/news/local/community/miami-dade/miami-beach/article253200228.html.

questionable to accomplish what seems unquestionably good to them. Means and ends are easily separated: biblical commands, ethical principles, and values may get substituted for a "whatever works" mentality.

Not so for the Improver. Healthy Ones are driven by two things: Goodness and Integrity. You don't let the rest of us cut corners, but make the right decision from day one in order to save everyone's lives. This is why I need Ones in my life!

The Biblical definition of integrity includes words like "soundness," "completeness," "upright," and "perfection."[2] Our English word integrity evolved from the Latin adjective *integer*, which we use to describe a whole number, as opposed to a fraction.[3] Ones desire to have an undivided heart—to have the wholeness of their ends be matched by their means; they always want the left hand to know what the right is doing. Healthy Ones stay true to their word no matter the difficulty of the decision, severity of the consequences, or whether anyone is watching. They consistently act in accordance with their worldview or moral code and are rarely guilty of showing any inconsistencies.

Your integrity is truly motivating and inspiring to us all.

In his letter to the Galatians, the apostle Paul recalled a time he called out Peter for lacking integrity. While in Antioch, Peter gave the Gentiles the impression he was comfortable eating with them (a sign of acceptance). However, when the more orthodox Jewish-Christian leaders showed up from Jerusalem, Peter distanced himself from the new Gentile converts, creating a rift in the fledgling community. Paul, who had worked so hard to bring these groups together, called out this duplicitous behavior, reminding Peter that such hypocrisy was out of step with the gospel.[4]

Like Paul, God has given you a gift to quickly notice situations of inconsistency so that you might help preserve the long-lasting structural integrity of your

---

2   W.L. Walker, "Integrity Definition and Meaning - Bible Dictionary," biblestudytools.com, accessed April 25, 2022, https://www.biblestudytools.com/dictionary/integrity/.

3   "Integrity: Meaning & Definition for UK English," Lexico Dictionaries, accessed April 25, 2022, https://www.lexico.com/definition/integrity/.

4   Galatians 2:11-14

family, organization, church, and society. If you acknowledge that God has wired you in this way and properly steward this gift, the world will have less moral and spiritual casualties. Like the Champlain Tower, all it takes is one bad choice to start down the path of ignoring integrity—eventually, the whole foundation crumbles and people are hurt in the process. Keep doing the small things everyday: setting out moral ends, defending ethical means, encouraging others to tell the truth and avoid white lies, and demonstrating what it looks like to keep your word and not make promises you can't keep. Lastly, do all of these things with a spirit of humility, staying on our level without any sense of superiority.

The Good News for Improvers is Jesus is the perfect example of integrity and is building a "spiritual house"[5] (the church) that will never crumble or fall. After His baptism, He went into the wilderness to fast for forty days and nights, and Satan came to Him at His weakest to try to break His integrity and get Him to fold. Though He was tempted in every way, Christ remained true.[6] Jesus did not cut any corners on His mission to rescue us, and in maintaining His integrity to the end, He opened the way for us to be whole as well. As an example for us, keep making good decisions, especially when no one is looking. Your integrity is truly motivating and inspiring to us all.

→ Pray

Father, when I'm tempted to take the easy way out, help me to respond like Joseph did after being tempted by Potiphar's wife: "How then can I do this great wickedness and sin against God?"[7] I promise to steward this gift of integrity to better protect myself and others in a world of moral and spiritual decay.

---

5   1 Peter 2:5

6   Hebrews 4:15

7   Genesis 39:9

Day 24 Reflections:

Describe a time when a situation tested your integrity. What helped you make the right choice?

_____

_____

_____

_____

When has integrity helped save you and those around you?

_____

_____

_____

_____

What can you do to cultivate integrity for those around you (teach a lesson, host a training, create new accountability measures, etc.)?

_____

_____

_____

_____

> ### → Respond
>
> Gently confront (or report) any unethical behavior you've been observing.

Day 25:

Focus of Attention

Finally, brothers, whatever is true, whatever is honorable, whatever is just, whatever is pure, whatever is lovely, whatever is commendable, if there is any excellence, if there is anything worthy of praise, think about these things.

—Philippians 4:8

JOHN MARK COMER, PASTOR AND BEST-SELLING AUTHOR, shared in an interview with Ian Cron that he has a sprawling forest behind his home in beautiful Oregon. But often, as he stands looking at the colorful natural beauty from inside his home, he can't help but see his dog's smudges on the window. This illustrates the tension that Comer and all Improvers feel: how are we supposed to appreciate the objectively beautiful when there is so much imperfection between us and it? As a child, Comer recalls getting into his perfectly made bed. He would lay awake for hours, trying to be as still as possible so as to not create any wrinkles in the covers. Ever since then, Comer admits,

> It doesn't have to be perfect to have peace.
>
> –John Mark Comer

as much as he longs to wake up to perfection, the whole world perpetually feels like an unmade bed.[1]

Ian Cron explains, "From the time they get up to the time they lie down, Ones perceive a world rife with errors and feel a bounden duty to correct it. There's no shortage of work to be done. Someone squeezed the toothpaste tube from the middle, the school secretary misspelled two words in the PTA newsletter, one of the kids didn't fold and hang their bath towel correctly, there's a fresh scratch on the car door, and the neighbors left for work leaving their trash cans at the foot of the driveway without the lids on. … Wherever they go, errors and mistakes jump out at them and yell, 'Fix me!'"[2]

We all see how hard you try. Many Ones, when asked what they want written on their tombstone, have shared, "He tried," or "She died trying."[3] We also see how much you help others. Jesus rebuked the religious leaders for laying heavy burdens on people's shoulders but not lifting even one finger to help, but not Ones![4] They are the teachers who stay after school to help struggling students, the parents who sit at the dining room table for hours helping their child with homework, and the pastors who get up early to study the Bible with their members. Ones do have high standards ("We can do better!") but will do *whatever it takes* to help others reach those standards—therein lies their greatest strength and its accompanying pitfall.

> We all see how hard you try.

When Ones start feeling an obligation to fix everything, their strengths become overdone and they end up looking like someone rigorously polishing a tiny scratch in the furniture, only to end up removing all the finish.[5] A real life example would be Apple's Steve Jobs, who used his extraordinary gifts to create beautifully flawless products and one of the most successful companies in history.

---

1   Ian Cron, "Part 2: Pastor John Mark Comer on Focusing His Attention (Enneagram One) [S03-018]," TYPOLOGY PODCAST (TYPOLOGY PODCAST, June 2, 2020), https://www.typologypodcast.com/podcast/2019/28/11/episode03-018/johnmarkcomer-part2.

2   Cron and Stabile, *The Road Back To You*, 95.

3   Wagner, *Nine Lenses on the World*, 165.

4   Matthew 23:4

5   Riso and Hudson, *Personality Types*, 396.

However, he was known by many for being harsh toward his employees, wearing them down on the road to the perfect product.

The Good News for Improvers is that you can better love others by redirecting your attention from what's wrong to what's right. Like Enneagram Sevens, (where you go in health), look at what is going right instead of what's wrong, seeing the glass as half-full rather than half-empty. Remind yourself of what John Mark Comer reminds himself everyday: "It doesn't have to be perfect to have peace."[6] The apostle Paul gives the command to fix our eyes on whatever is true, honorable, just, pure, lovely, commendable, excellent, and worthy of praise.[7] I can only imagine how hard this must be for you since God gave you the superpower of seeing the world in high-definition, where every blurry megapixel jumps off the screen and assaults your peace. But it's possible. Give yourself a break today, relieving yourself of an obligation to fix everything. God, not you, is responsible for every megapixel in your purview today.

➜ Pray

Father, You are worthy of praise for creating the world with unspeakable beauty and excellence. Forgive me for often focusing my attention on what's wrong and missing what is lovely and commendable. Thank You for giving me such a keen vision to notice what needs improving so that I can join You in making the world better.

---

6   Ian Cron, "Part 2: Pastor John Mark Comer on Focusing His Attention (Enneagram One) [S03-018]," TYPOLOGY PODCAST (TYPOLOGY PODCAST, June 2, 2020), https://www.typologypodcast.com/podcast/2019/28/11/episode03-018/johnmarkcomer-part2.

7   Philippians 4:8

Day 25 Reflections:

When has your "try harder" attitude helped someone else improve?

_____

_____

_____

_____

Describe what it feels like to see errors and mistakes everywhere you go.

_____

_____

_____

_____

What past mistakes or present flaws bring up feelings of disappointment? How will you remind yourself that it doesn't have to be perfect to have peace?

_____

_____

_____

_____

→ Respond

Do something "impractical" that doesn't improve your life but is fun and enjoyable.[8]

---

8   Christina S. Wilcox, _Take Care of Your Type: An Enneagram Guide to Self-Care_ (New York, NY: Tiller Press, 2021).

Day 26:

Thriving at Work

Then I said to them, "You see the trouble we are in, how Jerusalem lies in ruins with its gates burned. Come, let us build the wall of Jerusalem, that we may no longer suffer derision."

—Nehemiah 2:17

"JUST PRAY ABOUT IT." THESE WERE THE words I shared with my best friend in college after he came to my dorm room for some much-needed advice. Has anyone ever told you that? While it's true that prayer is absolutely essential, I have come to realize that telling someone to "let go and let God" is generally unhelpful and often causes more harm than good.

> You will not have a meaningful life without work, but you cannot say that your work is the meaning of your life.
>
> –Timothy Keller[1]

Nehemiah, the fifth century BC leader who supervised the rebuilding of Jerusalem was more of a practical God-follower. After hearing that Jerusalem's walls were broken down and its gates destroyed by fire, he sat down and wept

---

1   Timothy Keller and Katherine Leary Alsdorf, *Every Good Endeavor: Connecting Your Work to God's Work* (New York, NY: Penguin Books, an imprint of Penguin Random House, 2016).

for days—praying and fasting. But rather than waiting for God to send someone else, Nehemiah realized God wanted him to be the answer to his own prayer. He traveled to Jerusalem, secretly surveyed the rubble, and determined the size and scope of the project before committing to it. Then, to everyone's surprise, this cup-bearer got permission to rebuild from the king of their captors, Artaxerxes.[2]

Similarly, Improvers have the same incredible work ethic displayed by Nehemiah. As Cron and Stabile explain, "You not only want Ones to pilot your plane, you also want them to be the engineer who designs the brake system on your car, the pharmacist who fills your prescriptions, the programmer writing the code for your company's new website, the architect drawing up plans for your dream house, the accountant preparing your taxes and the editor combing through your latest book. And though I pray you never need one, you for sure want your cardiologist or neurosurgeon to be a One as well. Ones make top-notch lawyers, judges, politicians, military personnel, law enforcement officers and, of course, teachers."[3]

However, just like everyone, Ones have a few work pet-peeves. They don't like it when people break the rules, don't clean up after themselves, arrive late to meetings, miss deadlines, avoid responsibilities, ignore common

> Healthy Ones do their work out of pleasure, not out of a need to reduce anxiety.

courtesy, dismiss processes or procedures, share false information, deliver a poorly executed document or project, make excuses, or throw caution to the wind.[4] While many of these frustrations are valid, co-workers of unhealthy Ones become frustrated if they can't trust others enough to delegate, bog meetings and projects down in procedure and perfectionism, or try to control others with more guidelines and stricter accountability. Under distress, Ones may get very tense when discussing a point of disagreement and become unbending or critical, and

---

2 Nehemiah 1:3–2:8

3 Cron and Stabile, *The Road Back to You*, 104.

4 Chestnut, *The 9 Types of Leadership*, 64-65.

when they've had enough, they may completely withdraw and give others the silent treatment.[5]

Healthy Ones, though, do their work out of pleasure, not out of a need to reduce anxiety. They prioritize relationships over work and feelings over doing. They resist procrastinating out of fear they won't do it perfectly. As General George Patton said, "A good plan violently executed now is better than a perfect plan next week."[6] An influential One is someone who understands the difference between *requirements* and *requests*. Requirements are received by the team as "demands" whereas requests are received as an invitation. The first is a "command and control" strategy while the latter is an "inspire and align" strategy. Before you default to rules and structure, try inspiring us with your authentic emotions and vision for what's good!

The Good News for Improvers is though your labor in the home or workplace can be toilsome and frustrating, you'll be able to look back like Nehemiah and say, "for the good hand of my God was upon me."[7] The work Nehemiah set out to do appeared outrageous and was threatened at every step by corruption and malicious neighbors. And yet, God used Nehemiah to do more than his hurting people could ask or imagine during a time of despairing captivity. Working in the king's court, Nehemiah could have settled for comfort or control, but instead pursued courage and inspired others with a grand vision. Whatever challenges you are facing at work today, don't just "pray about it"—lean confidently into your practical gifts to accomplish more than you or anyone else thinks is possible.

→ Pray

Father, forgive me for settling for control when Your desire is for me to lead out with courage. Help me pray bigger, bolder prayers as I dream about best-case scenarios. Because you've given me incredible determination and practical gifts, use me today to inspire and align others to Your grand plan.

---

5   Ibid, 66-67.

6   William Cohen, *The Art of the Strategist* (New York, NY: AMACOM, 2004), 53.

7   Nehemiah 2:8

Day 26 Reflections:

Which workplace pet peeves listed above give you the most stress and why?

_____

_____

_____

_____

What requirements in your relationships and at work can you turn into requests? How can you use more motivating language?

_____

_____

_____

_____

How can you maintain a better work-life balance and not make work the meaning of your life?

_____

_____

_____

_____

→ Respond

Try to be less serious and have more fun at work. Make a joke, share a humorous story, bring your favorite food dish or drink, begin a meeting with an ice-breaker, or another fun idea to keep things light.

Day 27:

Let It Be

*Now Sarai, Abram's wife, had borne him no children. She had a female
Egyptian servant whose name was Hagar. And Sarai said to Abram, "Behold
now, the LORD has prevented me from bearing children. Go in to my servant;
it may be that I shall obtain children by her." And Abram listened to the
voice of Sarai.*

—Genesis 16:1-2

PAUL MCCARTNEY OF THE BEATLES LOST HIS mother to cancer in 1956 when
he was just fourteen years old. Ten years later, in the middle of a restless night,
his mother came to him in a dream and noticed that he was troubled. He remembers her saying to him very vividly, "Let it be." After waking up the next morning, McCartney took that feeling his mom gave him and wrote the song "Let It Be," which reached

> Be not angry that you
> cannot make others as you
> wish them to be, since you
> cannot make yourself as
> you wish to be.
>
> –Thomas à Kempis

number one on the Billboard Hot 100 and was later ranked by Rolling Stone #20 on The 500 Greatest Songs of All Time.[1]

The phrase "Let it be" just might be the mantra all Improvers need to live by. If there's one thing Ones think they need, it's control. It is very difficult for Ones to leave their world (and everyone in it) alone.[2] Just to be clear, I love that Ones think about everything. When my friend Raquel joined our church's staff team as our Director of Operations, my job became a lot easier as a pastor. Her sense of responsibility compelled her to take control of every aspect of the church. I slept better at night because of her leadership, and I love putting her systems into practice.

Ones take control because they want *good* outcomes. In their minds, everything will get off track or move in the wrong direction if they don't interject, but that is where Ones can get into unhealthy territory. They may push stronger adherence to rules and be perceived as over-controlling or may find themselves in power-struggles with co-workers; they may not delegate work or decisions if they aren't convinced it will lead to a good outcome.

> For the things God is not asking you to do today, just let it be.

After a long period of waiting, Sarah, Abraham's wife, didn't have any patience left for the son God promised, so she took control of the situation and decided to do something about it. She told Abraham, "Behold now, the Lord has prevented me from bearing children. Go in to my servant; it may be that I shall obtain children by her."[3] This common surrogacy practice strikes us as problematic for many reasons, but it was also not what God had promised. Abraham, ever the appeaser, went along with her request.

Are you tempted like Sarah to take control of the situation when nothing appears to be going right? When you are stressed, do you feel like you have to *do something*—whether that be cleaning the bathroom or calling another meeting?

---

1   Adam McDonald, "The Beatles - Let It Be: Lyrics & Real Meaning Explained," Justrandomthings, June 24, 2021, https://justrandomthings.com/2021/06/04/the-beatles-let-it-be-lyrics-true-meaning/.

2   Wagner, *Nine Lenses on the World*, 167.

3   Genesis 16:2

In those moments, ask yourself if you need to *let it be*. Don't become suspicious of God's sovereignty when things aren't going according to your plan or timetable. Your plans are better in God's hands: He's in control of everything. It's not your job to push the river but to jump in and trust the current.[4]

The Good News for Improvers is that, because of the resurrection, we know God is still in control! And if we want to follow this Sovereign Savior, it means we must relinquish all control over to Him—including the things we have zero control over. We have the Spirit to give us the wisdom we need to realistically know what we can or cannot control.

Practically speaking, this means letting others do things their way sometimes. If they want to clean the garage or landscape the yard in a certain way, just let it be. Remember that your way is just that: *yours*. Be careful not to overstep personal boundaries by giving others *shoulds* when they aren't willing to receive them. Think of the boundary between you and them like a door: if you ask permission to share, and the door is unlocked, go in—never force it open. And finally, Suzanne Stabile recommends that Ones ask themselves everyday, "What's mine to do?" Knowing what you shouldn't do is just as important as knowing what you should do. For the things God is not asking you to do today, just let it be.

→ Pray

Father, I praise You for providing the best possible outcomes for my worst-case scenarios. Forgive me for interjecting when I get tired of waiting for You to do something. Help me to let go of the felt need to control people and situations. When things aren't going according to my plan or timetable, remind me not to push harder but relax and just let it be.

---

4   Jerome Wagner, *The Enneagram Spectrum of Personality Styles: 25th Anniversary Edition* (New York, NY: Gildan Media LLC, aka G&D Media, 2021).

Day 27 Reflections:

Describe a time you wanted to take control of a situation but decided to just let it be. What was the result?

How have you tried to control or micromanage others? List some examples.

What situation are you tempted to control today? What do you fear will happen if you don't step in? How can you relinquish control to God?

→ Respond

To delegate without over-controlling, delegate the whole task rather than only a part. Discuss goals, time frames, and deliverables up front to achieve the best possible outcome, but then back off to allow them to succeed or fail. Do what only you can do and then leave the results to God.

Day 28:

Dealing with Resentment

He does not deal with us according to our sins, nor repay us according to

our iniquities. For as high as the heavens are above the earth, so great is his

steadfast love toward those who fear him; as far as the east is from the west, so

far does he remove our transgressions from us.

—Psalm 103:10-12

JESUS ENTERED A VILLAGE AND WAS WELCOMED into the house of his dear friends, Martha and her sister Mary. In first-century Israel (and much of the eastern world), people were judged by their hospitality, so Martha wanted to make sure she did everything right. While Martha's sister Mary was sitting at Jesus' feet talking with Him, she became "distracted by all the preparations that had to be made."[2] All it took was one glance at Mary, just sitting there

> If you hug to yourself any resentment against anybody else, you destroy the bridge by which God would come to you.
>
> —Peter Marshall[1]

---

1   Catherine Marshall, *A Man Called Peter: The Story of Peter Marshall* (Grand Rapids, MI: Chosen Books, 2002), 343.

2   Luke 10:40 NIV

oblivious to all the work that needed to be done, for the elder sister to verbalize her resentment: "Lord, do you not care that my sister has left me to serve alone? Tell her then to help me." Jesus replies, "Martha, Martha, you are anxious and troubled about many things, but one thing is necessary."[3]

This story, so often told, props up Mary as the hero, the calm, meditative one sitting at Jesus' feet—she was even complimented while her sister was lightly rebuked. But Martha doesn't get enough credit: after all, she opened up her home to Jesus, not Mary! Jesus was pleased with Martha's attempt to do her absolute best to serve her Lord and put her love into action. Like Martha, God sees the big heart behind all the "preparations" you do everyday and loves how you embody the incarnation through loving service. His wisdom for you is not to stop working entirely, but to do what is only yours to do, and then rest at His feet.

The *deadly sin* or *vice* of the Improver is anger expressed as resentment—either passively or overtly—for life not being "as it should be."[4] Do you suffer from low-grade anger caused by dissatisfaction with how things

> God holds no resentment toward His children.

are? Everywhere a One looks, things need fixing: someone is acting immature or breaking the rules, friends' homes are filled with countless undone repairs, their workspace is in disarray, details are getting missed, no one's done their chores yet—and that's just the tip of the iceberg. The worst thing of it all is *no one else seems to care.*

Do not think for a second that your battle with resentment makes you more sinful than anyone else. It's not easy constantly feeling the weight of how much the world needs improving. Much like Christ with His friend Martha, those who love you see your big efforts and even bigger heart. From that place of love, there are some proactive things you can do to reduce the anger that often leaks out sideways. Most Ones underestimate how much other people can feel their frustration despite their best efforts to hide it, and it leaves those around you walking on eggshells or feeling defeated.

---

3   Luke 10:41-42

4   See the appendix *Three Types of Improvers* in the back of the book for how each subtype responds to anger differently.

To become healthier, create better work boundaries. Limit the amount of responsibilities you assign to yourself so that you aren't exhausted all the time. Schedule a therapeutic massage or do stretches in the morning to release the body's tension. And because Ones don't like to let unjust actions go unpunished, they will also need to continually remember how much they've been forgiven and then release others from having to pay for their mistakes. Finally, it helps to get to the bottom of your anger by asking: Is there a value or principle of mine that has been violated? Is there something in how I see myself that is being threatened?[5] Keeping a journal or processing with a trained professional would be tremendously helpful for you.

The Good News for Improvers is God holds no resentment toward His children. None. "As far as the east is from the west, so far does he remove our transgressions from us."[6] Like Martha, let go of your resentment toward the "lazy" Marys in your life and sit at the feet of Him whose kind face has no trace of judgment. Because He's not angry with you, "do not let the sun go down on your anger."[7] Don't give the devil a foothold in your life. Like Jesus, let others come sit with you, knowing they don't have to be perfect to be in the presence of love.

→ Pray

Father, I praise You for holding no record of wrongs. The depth of Your mercy amazes me. Help me to forgive this unjust world filled with unfair people and come and rest at the feet of Jesus. Fill me with the Holy Spirit to say, "Father, forgive them, for they know not what they do"[8] when I start to keep an imaginary list in my head of others' mistakes.

---

5   Lapid-Bogda, *Bringing Out the Best in Everyone You Coach.*

6   Psalm 103:12

7   Ephesians 4:26–27

8   Luke 23:34

Day 28 Reflections:

What do you feel resentful about? In what ways do you currently feel annoyed with someone?

_____

_____

_____

_____

How do you let others know "without letting them know" you are angry?

_____

_____

_____

_____

How does it feel knowing Jesus invites you to come to Him daily, harboring no ill will against you for the things you did yesterday?

_____

_____

_____

_____

→ Respond

Perform a brain dump by writing down everything you are frustrated about right now. Honor your righteous anger but let go of the rest.

Day 29:

Structure Submits to Spirit

I am the vine; you are the branches. Whoever abides in me and I in him, he it is

that bears much fruit, for apart from me you can do nothing.

—John 15:5

STRUCTURES AND SYSTEMS HAVE A VERY IMPORTANT place in our families, churches, and almost any other organization—formal and informal alike. Improvers do not foolishly build on the sand but create blueprints for processes that can't be easily swept away. While others "go where the wind blows" and get caught empty handed like the foolish virgins who don't come prepared for the banquet,[2] Ones are thoughtful planners who think ahead, creating structures to facilitate healthier environments. Take the apostle Paul for example, who advised some ground rules for the church at Corinth when their weekly worship was getting out of control because too many people were

> Structures don't grow ministry any more than trellises grow vines.
>
> –Tony Payne and Colin Marshall[1]

---

1   Tony Payne and Colin Marshall, *The Trellis and the Vine: The Ministry Mind-shift that Changes Everything* (Sydney, NSW, Austrailia: Matthias Media, 2021).

2   Matthew 25:1-13

grabbing the microphone. In his mind, rules and structure reflect the God of order and peace and facilitate spiritual growth.[3]

In *The Trellis and The Vine*, authors Tony Payne and Colin Marshall compare a church's ministry structures to a trellis—wooden, fence-like structures made to support and display vine-growing plants. Payne and Marshall argue that while building the trellis is a necessary first step, the primary goal of ministry is to grow the *vine* (the people making up the kingdom), not the trellis. The structures exist to support and extend the true work of ministry, which is showing Christ—the living Word of God—to one another. Their big idea is that "structures don't grow ministry any more than trellises grow vines."[4]

Improvers must avoid the pitfall of becoming overly-reliant on structure to provide spiritual growth. Jesus said that apart from abiding in Him, the Vine, our hard work on the processes will all be for nothing. Franciscan priest and fellow One, Richard Rohr, points out that the key to understanding the balance of structure and Spirit, trellis and vine, is found in nature: "Whatever grows is not yet perfect, but it's on the way."[5] In Mark 4, we learn that the kingdom of God is like man who scatters seed upon the ground and then waits *patiently* and without interference for it to sprout and grow.[6]

> Structures were made for man, not man for structures.

God's creation is a marvelous organism, not a machine to control. Because we like to control nature to our advantage, manipulating all the variables so that we can predict perfect outcomes, it's tempting to do the same with our spiritual growth. But that's not how God works. Though we may have a step-by-step process for leading someone to the faith, at the end of the day, "The wind blows where it wishes, and you hear its sound, but you do not know where it comes from or where it goes. So it is with everyone who is born of the Spirit."[7]

---

3 1 Corinthians 14:26-33

4 Payne and Marshall, *The Trellis and the Vine*.

5 Rohr and Ebert, *The Enneagram*, 107.

6 Mark 4:26-29

7 John 3:8

Sailing is an activity that requires complete dependence on the wind (the Greek word for "wind," *pneuma*, is the same used for "spirit"[8]). Just as a trellis is necessary for a vine to grow, we must set the sails to catch the wind of the Holy Spirit. If we don't do the vital work of preparation, we won't be ready when the Spirit moves. However, greater dedication to the plan than to the Spirit is like overly-taut sails—the wind cannot adequately fill them, and you'll go nowhere. Ones must learn to wait for the wind and surrender their best-laid plans to the guidance of the Spirit.

The Good News for Improvers is, as Paul reminds us, God provides the growth,[9] so the pressure is off—we must build our trellises as securely as we know how and let the divine Vinegrower do His work.[10] Remember, structures (including those we believe to be scripturally-sound) were made for man, not man for structures. Keep trimming those sails, remaining aware of the *pneuma* piloting your course, so you are ready to pivot and move wherever it leads.

→ Pray

Father, no matter who waters or who plants, You cause the growth. Help me not to become so busy building the trellis that I forget to spend time abiding in You. Thank You for giving me the gift of building healthy structures to support kingdom work. I will trust Your Spirit over my plans and remain available and flexible for whatever You have next.

---

8   "G4151 - Pneuma - Strong's Greek Lexicon (CSB)," Blue Letter Bible, accessed April 26, 2022, https://www.blueletterbible.org/lexicon/g4151/csb/mgnt/0-1/.

9   1 Corinthians 3:6

10   John 15:1-11

Day 29 Reflections:

How has your trellis work supported the growth of your family, church, or workplace?

_____

_____

_____

_____

Are you spending more time cultivating the vine or building the trellis? What evidence do you have to support your answer?

_____

_____

_____

_____

Where do you need to become more flexible and hold your plans more loosely?

_____

_____

_____

_____

→ Respond

Mark off a day on your calendar to go somewhere new—ironically, plan to be spontaneous. Don't decide ahead what you'll do or prepare anything in advance. Just go with the flow and enjoy the wind filling your sails.

Day 30:

The Good/Bad Split

For our sake he made him to be sin who knew no sin, so that in him we might

become the righteousness of God.

—2 Corinthians 5:21

You probably hate living in the gray. An Improver's natural tendency is to bisect the world into "good" and "bad," light and dark, separating nearly everything into mutually-exclusive binaries. Paradox, doubt, and open-ended questions can make you feel itchy, while yes-or-no answers and right-or-wrong decisions are attractive because they minimize the "danger zone" gray areas of life and bring clarity. After a question has been thoughtfully examined by the One and the team reaches a decision after much deliberation, Ones rarely want to re-open the conversation if someone starts second-guessing the decision. To revisit the conversation feels like going back to the "dark" where ambiguity and moral confusion are lurking.

> The line dividing good and evil cuts through the heart of every human being.
>
> –Aleksandr Solzhenitsyn[1]

1   Daniel J. Mahoney, *Aleksandr Solzhenitsyn: The Ascent from Ideology* (Lanham, MD: Rowman and Littlefield, 2001), 50.

Ones can sometimes be guilty of "importing a strong moral framework to something others see as amoral."[2] For example, Ones may invoke a higher moral order to something as trivial as picking out a paint color for the living room or deciding on what kinds of meals others should or should not be eating. Turning open-handed issues into matters of moral conviction may make the One feel like sandpaper—instead of smoothing things out they can wear others down.

The perceived benefit of splitting the world into black-or-white categories is reducing stress. Splitting, a common defense mechanism used by Ones, attempts to extend control and therefore lessen anxiety's hold, but the result is almost always negative. You'll be amazed how often you naturally put your own self or preferences in the "good" category, while dismissing those you don't trust or understand into the "bad." Once you are able to locate the "badness," you can then distance yourself from it—an immoral leader, tainted theology, wayward church, or an unbiblical political party—of course, your leader, theology, church, or party automatically becomes the only "good" one!

But what happens when you find the "badness" within yourself or in your relationships? Will you reject yourself? Unfortunately, all too many Ones will do just that—or turn their self-loathing onto others. Does it sometimes feel as if you are in the wrong relationship altogether because good

> Others don't have to be perfect to be perfectly loved.

relationships should produce only good feelings?[3] In these situations, Ones need to remember that integrity, which they hold so dear, means holding space for *both* the good and the bad in yourself and others. When darkness surfaces and you make a decision to reject yourself or the relationship, you lose your wholeness, your integrity.[4] And it goes beyond relationships: good and bad are simply a part of life. There is doubt and uncertainty all around, and being angry at yourself or others for this fact will only make you miserable—and miserable to be around. This means not throwing away your past journals (real or metaphorical) filled

---

2 Drew Moser, *The Enneagram of Discernment: The Way of Vocation, Wisdom, and Practice* (Beaver Falls, PA: Falls City Press, 2020), 166.

3 Palmer, *The Enneagram in Love and Work*, 50.

4 Riso and Hudson, *Personality Types*, 410.

with past regrets and mistakes, but keeping them on the shelf, honoring them as part of the journey.

The Good News for Improvers is that the Father sent His Son Jesus to reconcile both the bad and the good within us on the cross: "For our sake he made him to be sin who knew no sin, so that in him we might become the righteousness of God."[5] The gospel allows us (and others) to be sinners and saints simultaneously. Thankfully, though good and bad still coexist within each one of us, God doesn't fall into splitting, withdrawing from us when our badness surfaces. Instead, like a skillful painter, He makes use of the many beautiful shades of gray in the world; like a surgeon, He operates gently and precisely on us with truth and grace. Because He treats you this way, you ought to be just as gentle with yourself and others, accepting that sin will always be an ongoing struggle in this life.

The next time your tendency to split kicks in and things seem either good or bad, right or wrong, set your strong opinions and first impressions on the shelf; become more curious. Ask others more "why" questions, listen longer than you think you need to, and know you could be wrong! And even when you believe you are clearly in the right, remember that others don't have to be perfect to be perfectly loved.[6]

→ Pray

Father, I praise You for covering me with Your goodness. Forgive me for attempting to put people into my good and bad boxes. Help me to be kind and compassionate toward those I disagree with or disapprove of. Give me the ability to have a both/and approach to life that sees beauty in the places and people I least expect.

---

5   2 Corinthians 5:21

6   Matthew Stephen Brown, *A Book Called YOU: Understanding the Enneagram from a Grace-Filled, Biblical Perspective* (Nashville, TN: W Publishing, 2021), 18.

Day 30 Reflections:

How does knowing that you don't have to be perfect to be perfectly loved make you feel?

_____

_____

_____

_____

When have you lovingly pursued someone even though there was much disagreement or disapproval?

_____

_____

_____

What are some ways you've done the good/bad split? How has this kept you from acknowledging goodness in all things?

_____

_____

_____

_____

→ Respond

To work on not polarizing, choose a world religion or political party different from your own and list three perspectives or practices that you can affirm as good.

Day 31:

You're Not Alone

[Elijah] said, "I have been very jealous for the LORD, the God of hosts. For the

people of Israel have forsaken your covenant, thrown down your altars, and

killed your prophets with the sword, and I, even I only, am left, and they seek

my life, to take it away."

—1 Kings 19:10

DO YOU EVER FEEL ALL ALONE—AS THOUGH no one else seems to care as much as you? Meet the prophet Elijah. The wicked rulers of Israel, King Ahab and Queen Jezebel, oversaw a land brimming with immorality, religious and social corruption, and pagan worship. Elijah's fierce loyalty to the Lord gave him the courage to host a showdown between the God of Israel and the prophets of Baal on Mount Carmel where, in a supernatural display of divine power, the Lord showed Himself victorious over the false gods. After Elijah had the false prophets seized and put to death, I'm sure he felt like he would finally get the spiritual revival he'd been waiting for.[1]

> Lonely is not a feeling
> when you are alone.
> Lonely is a feeling
> when no one cares.
>
> –Anonymous

---

1   1 Kings 18

Only, revival didn't come, and Elijah soon found himself on the run from a queen who publicly issued a death warrant. After he'd run all the way to Mount Horeb, he sat alone in a cave, feeling lonely and hopeless. Grieving, the Lord's prophet nearly despaired, crying out, "For the people of Israel have forsaken your covenant, thrown down your altars, and killed your prophets with the sword, and I, even I only, am left, and they seek my life, to take it away."[2]

Like Elijah, you too may find yourself alone after working so hard for broad-sweeping change, with little results. Under these stressful conditions, Improvers move to the low side of the Four personality type and begin to feel as if no one truly understands them, sees how hard they are working, or recognizes how much they've accomplished. They become withdrawn, moody, or melancholy and may start to dramatize what's happening, like the prophet Jonah under his wilted shade-plant: "Yes, I do well to be angry, angry enough to die."[3] The trademark self-control of Ones may spiral into secret feelings of envy and resentment: "Everyone else is having a better life than me."[4]

After so much work, despair can set in and their anger is no longer bent outward to productive action, but rather inward. When unhealthy Ones hit rock bottom, they often become excessively ascetic, seeking the control

> Even when you can't see it or feel it, God is still there.

they lack in the outer world through excessive diets or cleansing techniques, both "natural" and disordered (e.g. anorexia, bulimia, etc.).

Unhealthy Ones may also move the opposite direction, toward secretive indulgence, feeling justified in giving themselves secret "outs," or escape hatches. Some call this the "trapdoor phenomenon": Whereas some people go out the "back door" like the prodigal son, Trapdoor Ones stay put and lead a double life, acting on forbidden needs.[5] One example of trapdoor behavior is Attorney Eliot Spitzer, the New York Attorney General who crusaded against Wall Street

---

2   1 Kings 19:10

3   Jonah 4:9

4   Riso and Hudson, *The Wisdom of the Enneagram*, 115.

5   Palmer, *The Enneagram in Love and Work*, 43.

criminals and prostitutes to reform the city, yet later resigned after getting caught with a prostitute himself.

While trapdoor behavior might sound completely foreign to your experience, it's helpful to see how deep the rabbit hole goes if you neglect self-care, don't prioritize healthy outlets for pleasure, and ignore unacknowledged pain. When you feel loneliness and resentment beginning to set in, it's time to reach out to trusted mentors, non-judgmental friends, and licensed professionals. Also, knowing how common these responses are among your colleagues and friends can help you work to create cultures that include burn-out check-ins and offer resources to head off destructive responses before they set in.

The Good News for Improvers is that you're not alone. When Elijah fled into the wilderness, feeling alone and wanting to die, God sent an angel to put food and water by his head. Shortly after, at Mount Horeb, Elijah expressed the grief-filled fear that he was now God's lone follower, but it is at this moment that God famously spoke to him—not in the fire, the wind, or the earthquake, but in a gentle whisper, revealing that there were still seven thousand in Israel who had not bowed their knees to Baal.[6] Today, let this story be a reminder that you are not alone or abandoned; even when you can't see it or feel it, God is still there and is offering support and loving-kindness through those who are walking the path with you.

→ Pray

Father, open my eyes to see the countless ways You've supported me. Forgive me for believing I'm the only one who is trying. When I'm under pressure, give me the willpower to seek help rather than justify secret sin. Remind me that there are countless people who are working just as hard as me to see Your will be done on earth as it is in heaven.

---

6   1 Kings 19:18

Day 31 Reflections:

When have you felt all alone in your efforts to make positive changes?

_____

_____

_____

_____

What trapdoor behaviors have you given into in the past? What could have prevented you from going down that path?

_____

_____

_____

_____

How does Elijah's story give you hope? What God-given personal support (or like-minded people) might you be overlooking?

_____

_____

_____

_____

➔ Respond

Ask a friend or spouse to give you a half an hour each night to verbally process your day.

Day 32:

Grieving with Hope

But we do not want you to be uninformed, brothers, about those who are asleep,

that you may not grieve as others do who have no hope.

—1 Thessalonians 4:13

"JESUS WEPT."[2] THOSE WORDS REPEATED THROUGH MY lowered head as I sat at my desk, my own tears welling up. A long road of infertility had rocked my marriage, leaving crushed dreams and hopes deferred. Experiences like this are difficult for anyone, but when the ones from whom you seek comfort grieve differently, it can add alienation and loneliness to the pain.

> Because grief is not linear, you can't work your way through the stages, crossing them off a list as you go.
>
> –Adriel Booker[1]

For years, my wife, Lindsey, wept, believing we'd ever see the miracle we longed for—and to this day, still no miracle. I, on the other hand, didn't cry but instead kept telling her to have faith. Looking back, I can see now that what I had was not faith but naivety. (Sidenote: I have also come to see how hurtful it is to tell anyone who's struggling to simply

1   Adriel Booker, *Grace Like Scarlett: Grieving with Hope After Miscarriage and Loss* (Grand Rapids, MI: Baker Books, a division of Baker Publishing Group, 2018).

"have faith"; trite answers are never helpful, even if they are from Scripture.) While she cried, I suppressed my emotions by naively assuming everything would work out, but this was just an unconscious strategy to sweep things under the rug. In so doing, I suppressed Lindsey's pain, dodged her emotions, failed to offer the living presence of the Christ, and held fast to stoicism when I should have been sowing tears.

Thankfully, we joined a small group of believers who felt stuck in various ways. During one of our sessions, the leader pointed his finger at me and sternly said, "David was a man who grieved and was called a man after God's own heart. You haven't done that." Those stern words shocked me out of passivity, and the next morning, as I sat reading the story of Lazarus, I finally broke open. Coming across the powerfully short line, "Jesus wept," I heard God tell me: "Lindsey's tears are My tears." And for the first time since we began our struggle, I wept too.

The apostle Paul told the Thessalonian church that his desire for them was to grieve with hope. Do you struggle like me with the grieving part? In times of grief, Improvers are more likely to

> There is no right or wrong way to grieve.

stay busy with life, accomplishing things off the task list rather than sitting long enough with themselves to fully process their emotions. If any emotion arises, it is most often anger, which, though helpful in some circumstances, still ignores the injunction to grieve with those who grieve.[3]

Unanswered prayers (or "unfulfilled plans" as my One friend calls them) litter the pages of Scripture. Paul prayed for God to take away his "thorn in the flesh," but continued to suffer.[4] Lazarus's sisters asked Jesus to come right away, but He didn't.[5] Lindsey and I resonate with Zechariah and Elizabeth's story deeply, as they also struggled with infertility. They were "advanced in years," which means they experienced heartache for a very long time.[6] They must've been confused about

---

3   Romans 12:15

4   2 Corinthians 12:7-12 CSB

5   John 11:1-6

6   Luke 1:7

God's silence; after all, they were "walking blamelessly in all the commandments and statutes of the Lord."[7]

It would be a lot easier for all of us, especially for you as a One, to just do what God expects and know your prayers will be answered in return. This "do good, get good" mentality is a major theme in the book of Proverbs, but "do good, get good" is about probabilities, not absolutes. God in His sovereignty can choose to make exceptions to the rule to serve a higher purpose, one that we often cannot see.

The Good News for Improvers is that there is no right or wrong way to grieve. You don't need a step-by-step plan in order to grieve. Grief is not a DIY project; it's not something you can fix or just "get over." Rather, it's something you must *go through*. Perhaps today is the day to let go of the things you feel you "must" do and instead let your emotions breathe, clinging to the promise that "those who sow in tears shall reap with shouts of joy!"[8] Though the Bible is filled with righteous saints with unfulfilled plans on an individual level, it's clear that God's purposes are always fulfilled for His people. Zechariah and Elizabeth continued to serve God faithfully while they patiently waited, resisting the temptation to fall into despair and self-pity. Our story may not resolve as theirs did, but we commit to continue grieving with hope along with the saints of old, who longed for the fulfillment of God's promises, "saw them from a distance" and "greeted them."[9]

→ Pray

Father, I've often felt confused after praying to You but hearing no response. Give me the courage to keep pouring out my concerns to You with brutal honesty rather than fall into resentment. Empower me by Your Spirit to carry the burden of unanswered prayers and trust that You'll come through for me even if it's in a way I couldn't foresee.

---

7   Luke 1:6

8   Psalm 126:5

9   Hebrews 11:13 CSB

Day 32 Reflections:

What has grieving looked like for you in the past?

_____

_____

_____

_____

How have you observed yourself turning grief into a process? What is freeing about God allowing you to have a more natural, human reaction?

_____

_____

_____

_____

Which unanswered prayer has been the hardest for you to carry and why?

_____

_____

_____

_____

→ Respond

Write out your own prayer of lament using Psalm 22. What are you feeling (vv. 1-2)? What has been the most difficult part of the struggle? What do you want the Lord to do (vv. 19-21)? What praises will you proclaim (vv. 22-31)?

Day 33:

Thank You

Go to the ant, O sluggard; consider her ways, and be wise. Without having any

chief, officer, or ruler, she prepares her bread in summer and gathers her food

in harvest. How long will you lie there, O sluggard? When will you arise from

your sleep? A little sleep, a little slumber, a little folding of the hands to rest, and

poverty will come upon you like a robber, and want like an armed man.

—Proverbs 6:6-11

WE'VE COVERED SO MUCH GROUND IN THIS book already, yet I know Improvers tend to feel as though there's an endless list of possible improvements. But today, as we enter the homestretch, let's pause. Quite simply, I'm thankful for you, and for all the Ones in my life. As you think about who you'd like to become, I don't want you to lose sight of who you already are—a gift. Being responsible, you leave everything better than how you found it. Valuing excellence, you believe anything worth doing is worth doing well. When a meeting is scheduled,

> God has not called me to be successful; he has only called me to be faithful.
>
> –Mother Teresa[1]

---

1   James W. Kinn, *Teach, Delight, Persuade: Scriptural Homilies for Years A, B, and C* (Chicago, IL: Hillenbrand Books, 2009), 17.

you actually show up on time—although, as F.P. Jones humorously said, "The trouble with being punctual is that nobody is there to appreciate it."[2]

Thank you for denying yourself daily by prioritizing what's *right* over what's immediately pleasurable. You embody these words of Jesus: "If anyone would come after me, let him deny himself and take up his cross daily and follow me."[3] You are an example to us when you willingly deny your personal freedom to do what is good. As pastor and chaplain to the US Senate Peter Marshall prayed, "Lord Jesus, … Make us to see that our liberty is not the right to do as we please, but the opportunity to please to do what is right."[4]

You are the epitome of restraint, the definition of delayed gratification, constantly delaying personal rewards to pursue long-term, higher goals. And if you say you'll do something, you'll do it. It's not even a question. While many Christians focus on the first part of that old confessional prayer, "Most merciful God, we confess that we have sinned against you in thought, word, and deed, by what we have done," you are unique in turning our hearts and minds toward the last line: "and by what we have left *undone*."[5] You take to heart the words of the apostle James who said, "So whoever knows the right thing to do and fails to do it, for him it is sin."[6]

> God measures success by our perseverance, not perfection.

When it comes to the importance of Ones in the church, I can't put it any better than Pastor Matthew Stephen Brown: "Without [Ones], there's no church. Do you know why? Ones serve. They tithe. They come. They are faithful. Some people say, 'I don't know if we're going to go to church this weekend. I have to feel it.' But not Ones. They say, 'It is the Lord's day. We are going to church.' Thank God for the Ones."[7]

---

2   Tressider, Loftus, and Pollock, *Knowing Me, Knowing Them*, 48.

3   Luke 9:23

4   Peter Marshall, *Prayers Offered by the Chaplain, the Rev. Peter Marshall, D.D.: At the Opening of the Daily Sessions of the Senate of the United States during the Eightieth and Eighty-First Congress 1947-1949* (Washington, D.C.: U.S. Govt. Print. Office, 1949), 15.

5   Paul Victor Marshall, *Prayer Book Parallels: The Public Services of the Church Arranged for Comparative Study* (New York, NY: Church Hymnal Corp., 1989), 349.

6   James 4:17

7   Matthew Stephen Brown, *A Book Called YOU: Understanding the Enneagram from a Grace-Filled, Biblical Perspective* (Nashville, TN: W Publishing, 2021), 5.

Ones stand out in a world filled with lazy, unmotivated, unreliable people who waste their time and don't seem to care about improving themselves. It's been said that ants symbolize the hard-working nature of the One. In Scripture, Solomon tells us to "Go to the ant ... consider her ways, and be wise."[8] This tiny, tireless bug works through slow, small movements, storing up what it needs to last through the winter. The rest of us would do well to consider your work ethic and try to replicate even small parts of it in order to understand what it means to be a steward of God's grace and avoid physical and spiritual poverty.

The Good News for Improvers is that God will keep giving you perseverance to "run with endurance the race that is set before us,"[9] as you fix your eyes on Jesus, who endured on your behalf. I know you try harder than anyone else to be good but often get frustrated at the lack of progress, so cling to this promise today: "And let us not grow weary of doing good, for in due season we will reap, if we do not give up."[10] Remember, God measures success by our *perseverance*, not perfection. The presence (or lack of) spiritual fruit is not an indicator of your faithfulness: we labor but leave the results to God. We execute the small, daily steps of planting and watering, but in the end we will say, "God ... gives the growth."[11]

→ Pray

Father, forgetting what lies behind and straining forward to what lies ahead, I will press on toward the goal of fulfilling my calling in Christ Jesus.[12] I will rise today and run my race with endurance. Help me to forgive those who are lazy and wake up those who are in slumber. And as I work, remind me that I'm loved for who I am, not what I do.

---

8 Proverbs 6:6

9 Hebrews 12:1-2

10 Galatians 6:9

11 1 Corinthians 3:7

12 Philippians 3:13-14

Day 33 Reflections:

Which of the affirmations above most encourages you?

_____

_____

_____

_____

Where in your life do you feel weary and in danger of giving up? How does knowing God is responsible for the growth help you persevere?

_____

_____

_____

_____

Who in your life needs encouragement to keep going?

_____

_____

_____

_____

→ Respond

Write out any negative things your "inner critic" has been speaking over you. Read them aloud to hear how silly they are. Then replace them with true statements about who God says you are.

Day 34:

Discernment over Judgment

Let not the one who eats despise the one who abstains, and let not the one who

abstains pass judgment on the one who eats, for God has welcomed him. Who

are you to pass judgment on the servant of another?

—Romans 14:3-4

HAVE YOU JUDGED ANYONE IN THE LAST forty-eight hours? Perhaps your frustrating boss, the neighbor who doesn't care about their lawn, the lady in the check-out lane with rambunctious kids, or the guy texting and driving?

What about *yourself*?

> If you judge people,
> you have no time
> to love them.
>
> –Mother Teresa[1]

As Cron and Stabile point out, "Ones running on cruise control are mercilessly hard on themselves. Some demand perfection be maintained in only one corner of their lives (e.g., the yard, their boat, their office) while others apply it across the board. The house has to be immaculate, the

---

1   Gwen Costello, *Spiritual Gems from Mother Teresa* (New London, CT: Twenty-Third Publications/Bayard, 2008), 12.

written and posted the same day gifts are received. Ones have to keep hard copies of tax returns for five years to avoid being in violation of IRS rules."[2]

Ever since the garden, every personality type, when operating "in the flesh,"[3] makes an attempt to "be like God"[4] in some form or fashion. For Improvers, the temptation is to *take* the role of judge and conform others to their image of perfection, not God's. Unhealthy Ones take their God-given desire for goodness and become the interpreter of the law—defining what "should be" and then holding the world accountable to that vision.[5] When this occurs, chronic frustration marks the life of a One because nothing in this world seems to be good enough—including themselves.

Playing the role of judge also affects close relationships: Enneagram author Juanita Rasmus, as a One admitted, "The truth is that judging others has been at the basis of probably every major relationship interruption in my life."[6] My initial reaction to this incredibly bold statement is empathy because I know you as a One always see the log in your own eye before you see anyone else's splinter!

> God didn't judge us, but loved us into the beloved community of His kingdom.

At this point, you might be saying, "You're preaching to the choir here, but what should I *do*"? The answer is to cultivate discernment, which is the ability and wisdom to tease apart the varying strands of an experience or thought and to make individual, thoughtful decisions about each. Judgment is all too often an emotional reaction, whereas discernment takes the time to rationally break down and observe differences. Riso and Hudson advise Ones to be *witnesses*, not judges.[7] Witnesses observe the differences of opinion between two parties and the contexts in which they are shaped, but judges quickly make black and white decisions without much space for the nuances of life's greys. This doesn't

---

2 Cron and Stabile, *The Road Back to You*, 96.

3 Romans 7:5

4 Genesis 3:5

5 Vancil, *Self to Lose Self to Find*, 63-64.

6 Juanita Campbell Rasmus, *Forty Days on Being a One* (Downers Grove, IL: InterVarsity Press, 2021), 14.

7 Riso and Hudson, *The Wisdom of the Enneagram*, 121.

mean witnesses are ethical relativists, with every person's opinion carrying the same truth or weight, but they do have the humility to know they don't know everything and the wisdom to see that situations and facts change over time.

In the days of the early church, the apostle Paul told the diverse Roman house churches, now filled with both Jews and Gentiles breaking bread together, not to pass judgment on one another. Their baseline cultural values were different enough that, even though they shared a belief in Jesus, their fellowship could be torn apart by something as simple as what foods they felt free to consume. Whether one decides to eat meat or just vegetables, Paul says, both have their own good reasons before God for doing so; both are seeking to honor the Lord and give thanks in their own way, and it is therefore neither our business nor job to judge their choices: "So then," he tells them, "each of us will give an account of ourselves to God."[8]

The Good News for Improvers is God didn't judge us, but loved us into the beloved community of His kingdom. Jesus didn't stand in heaven, like the judgemental Pharisee who prayed, "God, I thank you that I am not like … ."[9] He came into our world and became the judge who put Himself on the hook for our faults. Even more, if anyone would be so bold to cast judgment in your direction, Jesus' Spirit, our advocate, would say to your accusers: "Let any one of you who is without sin be the first to throw a stone."[10] As one who is protected under grace, make this your motto today and write it down so you don't forget: "Mercy triumphs over judgment."[11]

---

8   Romans 14:12 NIV

9   Luke 18:11

10   John 8:7 NIV

11   James 2:13

→ **Pray**

Father, You are the most merciful Judge. Thank You for drawing me to Yourself not through fear, but with love. Forgive me for making rash judgements and give me greater patience and self-control to listen longer than I think I need to. Just as You put Yourself in my shoes by taking on flesh, help me to put myself in others' shoes to show greater empathy.

Day 34 Reflections:

Where have you been mercilessly hard on yourself and in need of grace?

_____

_____

_____

_____

Which of your relationships have been strained because of judging? Have you been trying to conform them to your image or God's?

_____

_____

_____

In your relationship with God, how have you experienced mercy triumph over judgment?

_____

_____

_____

→ **Respond**

Catch someone you know doing something right—and tell them why it means so much to you.

Day 35:

Words Matter

Death and life are in the power of the tongue, and those who love it will eat

its fruits.

—Proverbs 18:21

THE GREAT CHICAGO FIRE IN 1871 LEFT 100,000 people homeless, 17,000 buildings destroyed, 300 people dead, and $200 million worth of damage done. Though never confirmed, legend holds that the fire started when the O'Leary family's cow knocked over a lantern, setting the city's largely wooden infrastructure ablaze.[1] Though entire cities no longer burn down from a single lamp, the power of one spark can still set the world on fire. In his letter to the churches, the apostle James connects the potential power of our words to a spark: "So

> Words matter, and the right words matter most of all. In the end, they're all that remain of us.
>
> –John Birmingham

---

1 History.com Editors, "Chicago Fire of 1871," History.com (A&E Television Networks, March 4, 2010), https://www.history.com/topics/19th-century/great-chicago-fire.

also the tongue is a small member, yet it boasts of great things. How great a forest is set ablaze by such a small fire!"[2]

Improvers' tongues can be more flammable than most. An unhealthy One may start fires through speaking in a sharp, curt manner when pointing out faults; bringing up accusations from the past; or even through nonverbal cues like pursed lips and clenched jaws, piercing eyes, or a smile that all too clearly does not spell *happy*. Stress comes out sideways in the form of "I told you so," or "If you had only listened to me the first time." Ironically, when Ones express their anger at others, it's often coming from a place of being frustrated at *themselves* for not being perfect; the One's inner critic reserves the harshest words for themselves. The problem is, most of us don't know that.

Once you realize you've gone too far with your words—with others or yourself—there are some practical steps you can take. Start by confessing your mistakes to others: saying "I'm sorry"

> Be a coach rather than a critic.

out loud is a form of leading by example. Show others that you are perfectly human like the rest of us. Along these lines, try and catch yourself when you turn on "parent mode." There are four primary ways we communicate: adult-to-adult, child-to-adult, child-to-child, and adult-to-child. Out of all these strategies, psychologists have found that adult-to-child is the least effective way to communicate.[3] Therefore, do your best to speak on the same level with other adults while avoiding a parental tone.

Next, learn to pick your battles. Avoid zooming in on every blurry megapixel and providing criticism. Remind yourself that God is the ultimate Improver and will continue to make all things new in His timing. Another thing you can do is seek to balance clarity with kindness. Enneagram author Kim Eddy says Ones may believe clarity is synonymous with kindness: when things are unclear, people may suffer from a lack of direction. But the process of pursuing clarity without love and affirmation is easily taken the wrong way. Therefore, seek to mingle more warmth and compassion with your trademark directness.[4]

---

2 James 3:5

3 Riso and Hudson, *The Wisdom of the Enneagram*, 107.

4 Kim Eddy, *Enneagram for Beginners: A Christian Guide to Understanding Your Type for a God-Centered Life* (New York, NY: Penguin Random House LLC, 2020), 38.

Finally, seek to be a *coach* rather than a critic: "Let no corrupting talk come out of your mouths, but only such as is good for building up, as fits the occasion, that it may give grace to those who hear."[5] A critic focuses on what you did wrong, while a coach focuses on what you can do right. Critics take apart finished products, but coaches realize ninety-nine percent of life is lived in practice, where you are *supposed* to make mistakes! When you criticize someone, even when it's done constructively, you are making a "withdrawal." And if you make more withdrawals than deposits, over time the relationship will end up in the negative—which translates to increased stress and resentment. Coaches, however, seek to build relational equality rather than deplete it, leaving more than enough trust for well-timed, constructive feedback.

The Good News for Improvers is that Proverbs says life, not just death, is found in the power of the tongue.[6] Your words are honest, fair, sincere, polite, reasonable, and truthful. They don't just have the power to describe someone's reality, but change it forever. Your good words create a better world. In the huddle of this game called life, you are our coach pointing out the little things we did right and showing us how to improve our shot. You teach us how to play the game with integrity, win honorably, and lose with our heads held high.

→ Pray

Father, help me put away "anger, wrath, malice, slander, and obscene talk from [my] mouth."[7] I'm thankful that "The grass withers, the flower fades, but the word of our God will stand forever."[8] Your Word continually brings hope, assurance, and peace to my life. Give me life-giving words to say today to build up others in a way they'll never forget.

---

5 Ephesians 4:29

6 Proverbs 18:21

7 Colossians 3:8

8 Isaiah 40:8

Day 35 Reflections:

What is the greatest compliment or piece of encouragement you've ever received?

_____

_____

_____

_____

What point from today's reading stands out to you?

_____

_____

_____

_____

How can you be extra warm and kind in your speech or written communication moving forward?

_____

_____

_____

_____

→ Respond

Practicing confession is an important spiritual discipline for Ones. Though it will be emotionally painful, write your confessions down on paper. Then, write this absolution: "If we confess our sins, he is faithful and just to forgive us our sins and to cleanse us from all unrighteousness."[9]

---

9   1 John 1:9

Day 36:

The Discipline of Celebration

Bless the LORD, O my soul, and forget not all his benefits, who forgives all your

iniquity, who heals all your diseases, who redeems your life from the pit, who

crowns you with steadfast love and mercy, who satisfies you with good so that

your youth is renewed like the eagle's.

—Psalm 103:2-5

IMPROVEMENT IS THE PREFERRED FUEL FOR THE One, but the joy that comes from celebration is the longer-lasting fuel. When you accomplish something great, do you stop to acknowledge it or do you immediately move on to the next challenge? When something beautiful occurs in your or loved ones' lives, do you stop to take it in? When was the last time you created space in your busy schedule to celebrate past wins?

> The opposite of
> home is not distance,
> but forgetfulness.
>
> –Elie Wiesel[1]

My sons and I take frequent trips to the children's museum here in Omaha. My youngest son Zeke's favorite activity is the mining station. Like the goldpanners of old, he pours a bag of sand and rocks into the pan and

---

1 Chestnut, *The Complete Enneagram*, 57.

shakes it out until all of the sand is dumped into the stream underneath, leaving only the precious stones behind.

We all receive a mixed bag of encouragement and criticism every day, but sadly for a One, the precious encouragement often falls through the cracks, leaving them with only a bag of rocks. The human brain is generally biased toward critical thoughts, but in the Improver's life, this trait appears to be turned to eleven. That's why you, more than anyone, need to take inventory of the affirmations you receive so that you can silence the inner critic within.

When the discipline of celebration is neglected, we are training ourselves to believe that what we've done or experienced isn't important or worthwhile—the only thing that matters is the next milestone. Failure to pause and celebrate creates a cycle of feeling like we are never good enough and so we must rush on to the next task. However, when your spirit is alive with gratitude, you slow down from a human doing into a human *being*—becoming a life-giver to your family and workplace.

Enneagram author Christian Wilcox encourages Ones to cultivate gratitude by getting nostalgic: "Go through old scrapbooks and journals, reflect on how far you've come, and take note of how much you've actually grown. See all of the ways you've improved, all of the incredible changes and good efforts you have made; you are not a failure! Nostalgia can be good for [Ones] because of how much it enables them to see how hard they've worked and how much they've accomplished over the years. So turn on your favorite classic movie, bake your favorite recipe, invite over your oldest friend, and spend time reminiscing."[2]

> Failure to pause and celebrate creates a cycle of feeling like we are never good enough.

Human beings are prone to forgetfulness, which is why faiths across time and space have built up liturgies, or communal actions of remembrance, such as when Moses commanded the people of Israel, "Only take care, and keep your soul diligently, lest you forget the things that your eyes have seen, and lest they

---

2   Wilcox, *Take Care of Your Type*, 7.

depart from your heart all the days of your life. Make them known to your children and your children's children."[3] After miraculously crossing the Jordan, Joshua set up an altar and said, "When your children ask in time to come, 'What do these stones mean to you?' then you shall tell them that the waters of the Jordan were cut off before the ark of the covenant of the LORD. ... So these stones shall be to the people of Israel a memorial forever."[4] And of course, at his final meal, Christ set an example for His followers to actively remember Him through shared bread and wine.

Likewise, how will you lay your stones of remembrance? How will you gather and give thanks? How will you create more space in your life to actively remember God's provision and presence? Remember, the key to living with a serene mind and building more self-compassion starts with stopping to cultivate an attitude of gratitude.

The Good News for Improvers is that there is always something to celebrate. The psalmist exhorts us to "forget not" our God who forgives, heals, redeems, crowns, satisfies, and renews. You are magnificent to Him, and He has done great things for you and through you—all you have to do today is remember. Spend time writing in your journal today about how God has been faithful to you. Begin your personal conversations and team meetings today with the question: "Where have we seen God working?"

→ Pray

Father, You have forgiven my sins and redeemed my life from the pit. Your Son, Jesus, received a crown of thorns so that I would be crowned with Your steadfast love and mercy. With the Spirit's help, I will remember all You've done for me and model a celebratory life.

---

3 Deuteronomy 4:9

4 Joshua 4:6-7

Day 36 Reflections:

What are you celebrating today?

What has God done in your life that you will share with future generations? Name your stones of remembrance.

How can you schedule more time, personally or in meetings, to celebrate others?

→ Respond

Keep a record in your journal of all your stones of remembrance. Keep coming back to this list as a way to boost your self-confidence and future hope.

Day 37:

Behavior Modification

For God has done what the law, weakened by the flesh, could not do. By sending

his own Son in the likeness of sinful flesh and for sin, he condemned sin in the

flesh, in order that the righteous requirement of the law might be fulfilled in us,

who walk not according to the flesh but according to the Spirit.

—Romans 8:3-4

IN THE SEVENTEENTH CENTURY, A GROUP OF now-famous Improvers broke away from the Anglican Church, which in their minds was far too liberal, and sought to establish a more "pure" way of life in America. Like the Puritans, Ones carry a seriousness about sin that others don't seem to have—if this world could be composed into an orchestra piece, most of the world would sound too *flat* to the One when it comes to a concern for righteousness. But, an unhealthy One will overreact and turn *sharp* through an excessive concern for holiness—otherwise known as legalism.

> You cannot ask the
> law to do what only
> grace can accomplish.
> –Paul David Tripp[1]

1   Paul David Tripp, *Parenting: 14 Gospel Principles That Can Radically Change Your Family* (Wheaton, IL: Crossway, 2016), 45.

As we see in the book of Leviticus, out of a deep desire for holiness, God used purity laws (e.g., touch/don't touch, eat/don't eat) to use the physical world to explain spiritual realities. However, we are in a different chapter of history, and we also have something they didn't—the indwelling Holy Spirit. The temptation for puritanical Ones today is to go back to the days of Leviticus where it feels safer to cling to *laws* than lean on the Holy Spirit to navigate life's natural messiness.

Acknowledging this leaning in Ones is imperative because not everyone is motivated to be a good person by upholding mutually agreed upon norms. Understanding this dynamic will change *everything* about how you seek to motivate and change others. Jesus taught, "For it is from within, out of a person's heart, that evil thoughts come."[2] Jesus makes the case that all behavior flows from the heart. This is critical because, while the law may be able to suppress our behavior, it can't change our hearts. The state patrol can pull me over for breaking the speed limit but they can't turn me into a person who doesn't want to speed.

Timothy Keller asks, "Why do we lie, or fail to love, or break our promises, or live selfishly? Of course, the general answer is 'Because we are weak and sinful,' but the specific answer is that there is something besides Jesus Christ that we feel we must have to be happy. ... The key to change (and even to self-understanding) is therefore to identify the idols of the heart."[3]

> When your focus is on knowing Jesus, you'll spend less time fixated on your vice so you can spend more time cultivating virtue.

Our primary problem is not that we are weak sinners who need to comply more, but that we are strong worshipers who need to be redirected. Knowing this will help you relax your impulse to go "sharp" and push "common sense" onto others, creating more *shoulds*. While firmly saying things like "stop it" or "obey" is necessary to protect and redirect young children, it becomes insufficient as we get older. Asking heart-level questions to find out why someone is breaking the rules is necessary to help them break free of their idols.

---

2   Mark 7:21 NIV

3   Timothy Keller, *The Prodigal God Discussion Guide: Finding Your Place at the Table* (Grand Rapids, MI: Zondervan, 2009), 76.

Behavior modification only focuses on surface actions, but looking to the heart helps us seek the Spirit for transformation. Trying to stop our addictions through behavior modification is like mowing the weeds: they'll just come back again! It's only when we let go of our old desires and replace them with more powerful ones that we'll grow into our new self.

The Good News for Improvers is that "God has done what the law, weakened by the flesh, could not do."[4] Though the law is a helpful guardian in learning God's will,[5] its primary purpose was always to point us to Christ, the only One who can truly change our hearts. This gives new meaning to the old saying, "a good lawyer knows the law and a great lawyer knows the judge."[6] When your focus is on knowing Jesus, you'll spend less time fixated on your vice so you can spend more time cultivating virtue. By beholding Him, rather than focusing on what you or someone else should do, you will be changed from one level of maturity to another.[7] And through the Holy Spirit, you will become someone who honors the spirit of the law without being enslaved to its letter. As you do, you'll become someone who is perfectly in tune, drawing others to joyfully obey as they hear you playing the music of the gospel in your own life.

→ Pray

Father, thank You for giving me the grace and power to change. Help me let go of the belief that pushing people to obey the rules will actually change them. Give me wisdom to understand the ways of the human heart so I can point myself and others to find fulfillment in You. I know You will give us the desires of our hearts if we delight ourselves in You.[8]

---

4   Romans 8:3

5   Galatians 3:24

6   J. Michael Martinez, *The Greatest Criminal Cases: Changing the Course of American Law* (Santa Barbara, CA: Praeger, an imprint of ABC-CLIO, 2014), 56.

7   2 Corinthians 3:18

8   Psalm 37:4

Day 37 Reflections:

How has behavior modification or "Christian accountability" hurt or helped you on the journey?

_____

_____

_____

_____

What should you change, knowing obedience to the law (or holding someone accountable) is not the end, but a means to a better end?

_____

_____

_____

_____

Are you putting more energy right now into stopping your vices or cultivating virtue? How do you know?

_____

_____

_____

_____

→ Respond

Begin practicing one of these spiritual disciplines to proactively cultivate virtue: meditation, prayer, solitude, fasting, study, service, confession, or celebration.

Day 38:

Productive Prioritizing

For we are his workmanship, created in Christ Jesus for good works, which God

prepared beforehand, that we should walk in them.

—Ephesians 2:10

TECHNOLOGY WRITER COLIN ROBINSON ONCE DISCUSSED THE difference between efficiency and effectiveness. He explained that many people are great at being efficient: completing many tasks quickly and with little effort. But like using a high-efficiency LED porch light during the day, their efficiency didn't lead to tangible effects. It may be smart to replace an old incandescent bulb with an LED light bulb, but its light is only useful in the dark.

> **The most unproductive thing of all is to make more efficient what should not be done at all.**
>
> –Peter Drucker[1]

Ones are confident, hard-working people who—given the right context—can turn their drive and effortless efficiency into actual effectiveness. Being efficient is about "doing things right," which is of ultimate concern for the One, but being *effective* is about

---

1 Matt Perman, *What's Best next: How the Gospel Transforms the Way You Get Things Done* (Grand Rapids, MI: Zondervan, 2017).

"doing the right things." Accomplishing more tasks in the least amount of time may just mean you've created extra space to do more of the wrong things! Ones can also fall prey to the "Improvement Paradox," where their fixation on improving so many things can keep them from doing the one right thing needed for personal or professional growth.

Enneagram author Sarajane Case mentions that while Improvers are very efficient, they become ineffective when they constantly seek to perfect *unnecessary* areas. Therefore, Case advises Ones, "Get really honest with yourself about where you are expending energy unnecessarily, that could be going into the relationships that you want to preserve or the projects that are most important to you. It can seem unnatural to prioritize your

> Being efficient is about "doing things right," ... but being effective is about "doing the right things."

energy in this way. However, once you start to notice it, you can see how you are giving everything in your life equal weight—treating the re-organization of your computer desktop with the same perfecting weight as you do the person who is asking you to consider how you've hurt their feelings."[2]

Because Ones are driven, high-energy performers, they will always be in demand by the people around them. But having the potential to do many things well often leaves Ones feeling the pressure to do it all. And when you care about everything, you won't care about the next *right thing*. Therefore, you must learn to let go of priorities, tasks, and decisions that belong to others and listen to God's specific assignment for you today.

How do you sort out the good works God has prepared for you from the other things you would merely be efficient in? The answer is: know what the next right thing is and do it first. To do this, you can't just rearrange all the urgent tasks that arise in the whirlwind of life on sticky notes—you must control your schedule before your schedule controls you. As productivity guru Stephen Covey says, "The key is not to prioritize what's on your schedule, but to schedule your priorities."[3] As a Christian, our first priority is to love God and others. True,

---

2   Case, *The Honest Enneagram*, 42.

3   Covey Stephen, *7 Habits of Highly Effective People* (New York, NY: SIMON & SCHUSTER LTD, 2004), 161.

Christlike productivity means prioritizing people over projects, but you can see the struggle here, right? Loving others doesn't mean doing what's theirs to do. As we've discussed before, you must keep asking the question: What's *mine* to do? Loving others today might mean delegating responsibility to them.

Jesus could have become more efficient in His ministry, optimizing it for the greatest impact in the works of healing, feeding, and teaching; or He might have followed the crowds' desire and become a king. But He denied these wishes and actively fled from them. That was because the good works He accomplished were not His primary task—they were merely stopping points on the way to Jerusalem. He didn't let stopping to improve everyone and everything get in the way of doing the one *right thing* that the world needed the most.

The Good News for Improvers is that we have the Spirit of Jesus to help us discern the path of most effectiveness. If you carve out time to sit in the presence of God this week, you only have to wait for Him to say, "Follow me." Spend time bouncing your priorities off of your loved ones and those in your church or community. With their help, you'll have all the wisdom you need to discern what's most important on your list. You don't have to fret over knowing the next ten steps. You just have to know the next right thing.

→ Pray

Father, I get distracted by all the things that need getting done. It's hard to stay focused on what's most important. But when I look at Your Son, Jesus, I see a Man with focus. He often had to tell people no in order to stay on task and show love to many. He filtered everything through loving You and loving people. Give me that same focus. Tell me what to do next. I'm listening.

Day 38 Reflections:

How did Jesus pursue effectiveness over efficiency in His ministry?

_____

_____

_____

_____

To be more effective, what are you doing efficiently that you should be delegating?

_____

_____

_____

_____

What next right thing is God asking you to do that you keep avoiding through busy work?

_____

_____

_____

_____

➜ **Respond**

Write down a rough draft fifty-word personal mission statement that will help you prioritize your future pursuits.

Day 39:

Express Yourself

I cry aloud to God, aloud to God, and he will hear me. In the day of my trouble

I seek the Lord; in the night my hand is stretched out without wearying; my soul

refuses to be comforted. When I remember God, I moan; when I meditate, my

spirit faints. You hold my eyelids open; I am so troubled that I cannot speak.

—Psalm 77:1-4

HAVE YOU GIVEN SOMEONE THE "YES NOD?" You know what I mean—it starts with a friend or co-worker passionately sharing an opinion that evokes an emotion deep within. Without even having to think about it, you come up with something heartfelt to say, but for some odd reason, you restrain yourself and give a rational response instead.

> Wrestling with God is a sign of intimacy. You can't wrestle with someone you're far away from.
>
> –Jon Acuff

Average to unhealthy Improvers may forfeit many opportunities in life to express their true emotions because of strict external or internal standards. Whereas Eights give free reign to their gut instincts and Nines are often out of touch, Ones try to reign these instincts in, which keeps them from full and free expression.[1] Whenever an impulse arises, Ones run it through a "quality control" filter, and many of these feelings get left on the chopping block if they are deemed inappropriate. Therefore, the path of growth for you is learning how to express, rather than repress how you really feel. Healthy change requires shifting from "evaluation mode" to "expression mode"—whereby you stop over worrying about what's acceptable and unacceptable and just be your true self.

Being a pastor, I think there is a stronger temptation when others are around me to put on a mask when they are grieving the loss of a loved one. I hear things such as, "I'm doing good. I know God is going to get glorified through all of this." I want to respond, "He surely will, but He also cares about your heart." God desires authenticity over appearance, but this is easier said than done. As a Three who struggles with expressing emotion myself, I must confess that the emotive Psalms was my least favorite book of the Bible for years. It has taken a lot of time and effort to replace my "well-worded requests" with raw emotion, and I'm often still tempted to fear God's punishment if I say what I *really* feel (as though He doesn't know). Can you relate? I read Psalm 77:1-4 and still ask myself, "Can I actually say those things to God and not be judged?"

One of the foundational tales of the Hebrew people is Jacob's wrestling match with God at the Jabbok River. As darkness fell, an "Unknown Traveler" wrestled with

> God desires authenticity over appearance.

Jacob as he lay near the water's edge, and there they struggled until the horizon began to brighten. Suddenly, this Unknown Traveler, who we discover represents God, "touched" Jacob's hip socket, wrenching it out of joint. In a surprising twist, Jacob—the quintessential trickster and runner—had finally been backed into a corner and found the courage to engage. God says, "Let me go," but Jacob replies, "I will not let you go until you bless me." Then God responds, "Your name shall no longer be called Jacob, but Israel, for you have striven with God and with men, and have prevailed."[2] Israel, God's chosen people, fundamentally believed God delights in those who aren't afraid to strive and struggle with Him.

---

1   Riso and Hudson, *Personality Types*, 378.

2   Genesis 32:26-28

The Good News for Improvers is that God loves those who wrestle with Him and express what they truly need and feel. Take comfort in the fact that you can find relief today by releasing all of the energy you've been holding back and letting God have it because He can handle and actually desires it. As Jon Acuff says, "Wrestling with God is a sign of intimacy. You can't wrestle with someone you're far away from."

Jesus Himself was a kaleidoscope of emotions, able to express the entire spectrum of human warmth and love, anger and frustration, grief and loss. When we say that Jesus was "fully human," we mean He plumbed the depths of the human experience and expressed His true self. In a moment of raw honesty in the garden before His death, Jesus prayed, "My Father, if it be possible, let this cup pass from me."[3] He showed us that living with real integrity means being open and honest about our vulnerabilities, not giving others the impression that we are *more* than human.

→ Pray

Father, I admit that I sometimes hesitate to bring my true emotions out into the open. Thank You for giving me the opportunity to pour out my heart to You with brutal honesty. I praise You for making allowances for both the good and bad feelings that arise within me. Give me the courage to set an example of authenticity for those around me today.

---

3   Matthew 26:39

Day 39 Reflections:

Was "wrestling with God" encouraged or discouraged in your church growing up? What about now? Explain.

_____

_____

_____

_____

When have you sought to draw emotional truths out into the light? Did it go well or poorly? Explain.

_____

_____

_____

_____

What can you do to shift your paradigm from evaluating to expressing?

_____

_____

_____

_____

➜ Respond

Do something creative and give yourself time, space, and permission to express yourself through that medium without evaluating or judging yourself. Pretend that there's nothing wrong with it and see how it feels.[4]

---

4   Chestnut, *The Complete Enneagram*.

Day 40:

The Good Life

You make known to me the path of life; in your presence there is fullness of joy;

at your right hand are pleasures forevermore.

—Psalm 16:11

I'VE SPENT MY WHOLE LIFE HERE IN Nebraska, whose state slogan boasted "the good life." I won't deny there are many great things about my home state, but if we're honest, most people here don't know anything different. I wouldn't blame someone on the coast for being a bit skeptical about the idea of giving up everything to move here, hoping to find a higher standard of living in this humble Midwest state.

> **Love God and do whatever you please: for the soul trained in love to God will do nothing to offend the One who is Beloved.**
>
> –Saint Augustine[1]

I want to finish this incredible 40-day journey by revisiting your version of the good life. One could boil this entire book down to one piece of advice: *let God redefine your definition of good.* If you haven't noticed, you are very different from others!

---

1 Neil Cole, *One Thing: A Revolution to Change the World with Love* (Nashville, TN: Thomas Nelson, 2016), 31.

The good life for many people means indulging in the pleasures of this world, pursuing individual happiness, and running from anxiety through escapism, but for you, it means self-denial, doing your duty, and working harder.

What I'm about to say may sound heretical to you as One, but your mission must be to figure out what you *want* to be doing, not what you think you *should* be doing. Case in point: Andre Agassi, one of the greatest tennis players of all time, said, "I play tennis for a living, even though I hate tennis, hate it with a dark and secret passion, and always have."[2] This quote is from his autobiography, *Open*, where he divulges that the only reason he ever played tennis was because his father thought he should.

Much like the tennis legend, Ones may get to the end of their lives with the realization that they were only doing what they (or others) thought they should be doing. They realize

> **Let God redefine your definition of good.**

they pursued the career that made more "logical" sense or the one their parents wanted them to do, so let me ask you: are you doing what you love? I'm not talking about reducing anxiety by accomplishing another thing off the checklist; I'm talking about finding *pleasure* in all that you are doing.

The One's version of the good life is like docking in a harbor where all the ships are neatly ordered and everything feels under control. But their future destination is put on hold because there are too many logistical problems to sort out and maintenance to be done. Because of their good hearts and practical gifts, Ones may even be asked to stick around long-term to help manage, lead, and improve the harbor's operations, which may even give them a great sense of purpose and fulfillment. But deep down, they know it is not the *best* life.

God is calling you to lift up your anchor and set out into the deep—a thrilling journey filled with spontaneous surprises, laughter, optimism, open-mindedness, and deep curiosity. On this wild ride you can watch perfect sunsets and starry nights, enjoying every moment as it comes rather than running it through your quality control filter. If you are able to get your mind off of what needs perfecting in the harbor, and lift your gaze toward your future, you'll see that God has more

---

2   Andre Agassi, *Open: An Autobiography* (New York, NY: Alfred A. Knopf, a division of Random House Inc., 2009), 3.

for you ahead on the open sea. Remember this: His *glory* and your *good* are not at odds with each other, rather they are two sides of the same coin. God wants to give you the desires of your new heart because those desires are actually on loan from Him.

The Good News for Improvers is God has chartered a course where joy and pleasure await you, not placed you on an ascetic path whereby you have to practice extreme self-discipline and avoid all forms of indulgence. As David sings, "You make known to me the path of life; in your presence there is fullness of joy; at your right hand are pleasures forevermore."[3] Take note that joy is found in God's presence, not your tasks. If C.S. Lewis had known the Enneagram, I think he'd say that Ones are far too easily pleased with perfecting mud pies in the slum rather than joining God for a walk on the beach.

Remember, you are God's beloved, and He came that you may have the good life and have it abundantly. So take a walk with Him today, be yourself, laugh, and "taste and see that the Lord is *good*!"[4]

→ Pray

Father, I praise You for inviting me into a story that is better than any I could've written for myself. Give me the courage to pick up my anchor and follow Jesus into uncharted waters. Help me to discern between what I think I should do and what You want me to do. As I await heaven's joy, I will delight myself in You as I fulfill all my responsibilities here on earth.

---

3 Psalm 16:11

4 Psalm 34:8

Day 40 Reflections:

How has God redefined your definition of good?

_____

_____

_____

_____

What would you love to do if you felt free to pursue it and experienced no guilt in doing it?

_____

_____

_____

_____

How do you want the world to remember you?

_____

_____

_____

_____

➜ Respond

Find a life coach or spiritual mentor to come alongside and support you in accomplishing your goals. Start working courageously toward something today that seems impossible without God's supernatural power and grace.

Prayer for Improvers

FATHER, I AM DEEPLY GRATEFUL TO YOU for creating me in Your image as Your beloved child. You created me to specifically reflect Your goodness and desire for perfection. I confess that my self-created standards have left me frustrated, overwhelmed, and overworked. I have found myself at times inflexible, critical, judgmental, demanding, and resentful. You, being rich in mercy, saw me from heaven and sent Your righteous Son, Jesus, to die on the cross for all my imperfections. Now, I revel in the fact that You will never condemn me and always provide unending grace and patience. Clothed with the power of the Holy Spirit, I will view serenity not as improved circumstances, but as letting go of all control, trusting that You are making all things new. Putting off anger and resentment and putting on my new self that is made in Christ's image, I will pursue progress over perfection, curiosity over judgment, grace over grudges, and joy over seriousness, knowing I don't have to be perfect to be perfectly loved.

Three Types of Improvers

BELOW IS A SUMMARY OF THE THREE types of Ones (called subtypes) from the teaching of Beatrice Chestnut, whose book, *The Complete Enneagram* covers all twenty-seven subtypes of the main nine Enneagram types.[1] As discussed in the introduction, these subtypes are helpful in drilling down the different nuances of the Improver.

Warning: many of these descriptions will seem overly negative. However, one of the main purposes of the Enneagram is to help us discover our "shadow self"— the ways we interact with the world unconsciously and often in times of stress. These descriptions are not indictments; rather, they are a further opportunity to deepen our awareness of how to interact with the world.

The Self-Preservation One

The Self-Preservation One is responsible, reliable, and trustworthy, repressing their anger more than the other two subtypes. Believing a "good" person doesn't show anger, they become outwardly warm, virtuous, tolerant, forgiving, and sweet. The anger of this subtype manifests as good intentions, obedience to rules, and an obsession with "doing it right." Though they are the best at controlling their anger, it may leak out as irritation, frustration, or resentment. This subtype worries the most, which leads them to forecast problems and plan out everything perfectly. They feel there is always so much to be done and can't relax or release themselves from a project until everything "feels" under control. The most perfectionistic of the subtypes, these Ones are extremely hard on themselves when they don't get it right and are the most sensitive to being criticized. They are quicker to own up to their failings and forgive generously when others admit they dropped the ball. The Self-Preservation One gets confused with Sixes because of their black-and-white thinking, obedience to rules and authorities, and an underlying sense of worry. However, while Sixes are preoccupied with coping with their anxiety and looking externally for guidance, Ones are preoccupied with getting things right and have their own internal moral compass.

---

1 Chestnut, *The Complete Enneagram.*

The Social One

The Social One tends to be a cooler, confident, more intellectual type. They aren't as perfectionistic but rather serve as our role models who strive to be the perfect example. They want to teach others the right way to be, think, and behave. Thus, this subtype can have a "school teacher" mentality with very high standards in their relationships. It's as if they are implicitly saying, "Let me teach you how things are or should be." Their anger is only half-hidden and manifests itself as overconfidence because they are convinced they are the "owners of the truth." Being confident they are right, it becomes nearly impossible to convince them of your point of view. They have an underlying need to point out where others are wrong so they can stay in control of the situation. This can make them appear superior to others or a "know-it-all," although they might not be aware of this. The Social One may resemble a Five because they can be more introverted, emotionally detached, self-sufficient to the point of not needing others, and feel uncomfortable in groups. However, Ones readily engage the world every day to improve it, while Fives focus primarily on conserving their energy and resources.

The One-to-One One

While the Self-Preservation One appears warm and the Social One cool, the One-to-One One character is "hot" with zeal. They bring energy and intensity to all their relationships. They are the countertype because they allow their anger to come to the surface and don't suppress their instincts as much. They may break the rules, assert their will over others, or go after what they want if they believe God is on their side. Whereas the Self-Preservation One is a perfectionist and the Social One the perfect example, the One-to-One One feels as if they are the chosen "One" to perfect the world. They focus less on perfecting themselves and more on broad-sweeping reformation. This subtype can be impatient, intense, passionate, idealistic, and compelling. They may have the mentality of a conqueror and rationalize their zealotry because of their adherence to a higher calling or moral code. The One-to-One One may look like an Eight because they are energetic, strong, assertive, confident, determined, not afraid of confrontation, have a "go for it" mentality, and impose their vision on others in an attempt to make the world a better place. However, Ones are "over-social" while Eights are generally "under-social."

Next Steps

I'M SO PROUD OF YOU FOR FINISHING this 40-day journey. I know you might be feeling the gamut of emotions right now. Being "seen" can feel scary. Therefore, I want to remind you that *you don't have to be perfect to be perfectly loved.* God knows how hard you are on yourself and wants you to close this book hearing His voice and not your inner critic. He can't love you any more (or less) than He does right now. He's taken responsibility for you and will be with you every step of the way from here on out.

You're probably wondering: *What now? My eyes have been opened, I've grown in greater self-awareness and empathy, and now I'm ready to take the next step!* Here are some ideas:

1. Follow "Gospel for Enneagram" on Instagram, Facebook, or Twitter to continue learning and engaging.

2. Download my free resource called *Should Christians Use The Enneagram?* at gospelforenneagram.com.

3. If you found this book helpful, please leave an honest review (or star rating) online or share on social media so others can find it.

4. Visit my website, gospelforenneagram.com, to find more helpful links and resources.

5. Join a church community where you can continue to grow in your knowledge of God and self. To go the distance, find a mentor, coach, or support system.

6. Ask a friend, spouse, or mentor to meet regularly with you to discuss the insights God has revealed to you through this book. Invite them, along with your small group, to get a devotional on their Enneagram type and share what they learn with you.

7. Email me with any thoughts, questions, or feedback to tyler@gospelforenneagram.com. I'd love to hear from you!

Acknowledgements

My wife: Lindsey, you show me the gospel every day by loving me for who I am and not what I do. Thank you for your tremendous encouragement to be a writer and for bearing with my workaholic tendencies. I want to be more like you.

My editors: Lee Ann, your veteran experience and thoroughness increased the value of this book tremendously. I know it was tremendously challenging as a One to perfect my book while being reprimanded for being a perfectionist! This whole project took tremendous courage. I hope you know this book is more excellent because of you. Joshua, thank you for bringing your incredible creativity to the table. Your re-rewrites helped elevate my writing to a whole new level. Stephanie, your attention to detail and passion for this project gave me tremendous confidence.

My coach: John Fooshee, thank you for your Enneagram coaching and partnership. I'm deeply grateful for your willingness to come alongside me and put wind in my sails.

My influences: I wouldn't have been able to pull this off without a multitude of direct and indirect influences such as pastors, teachers, and writers (including you, mom!) over the years. I'm deeply grateful for the spiritual heroes that have come before me and shaped me.

www.GospelForEnneagram.com

Follow us:

 /GospelForEnneagram

 @GospelForEnneagram

 @GospelForGram

Made in the USA
Columbia, SC
06 October 2022